THE J. PAUL GETTY MUSEUM

Los Angeles

Ancient
HERBS

Marina Heilmeyer

Contents

INTRODUCTION

The eruption of Vesuvius on 24 August in the year A.D. 79 engulfed one of the largest, richest, and no doubt most impressive villa gardens that had adorned the slopes of the volcano. The various garden zones were part of an estate situated outside the city walls of Herculaneum. Its interior rooms opened onto terraces and porches that afforded views of garden installations and water displays against a scenic landscape composed of the picturesque Gulf of Naples and the estate's vineyards, olive groves, and a vegetable garden.

The luxurious villa was rediscovered in the eighteenth century. Because of the many charred book scrolls found there, the excavators gave it the nickname "Villa dei Papiri." They were unable to exhume more than a part of the destroyed courtyards and building complexes buried beneath hardened layers of mud and lava, and even today excavation remains incomplete.

Far from Herculaneum in place and time, on the California coast at Malibu in the 1970s, the original magic and former beauty of these structures were restored to life in the form of a replica. The sea view, mild climate, and southern light all help create a perfect illusion. Just as in the time of the Roman emperors, the peristyle and courtyard gardens are filled with evergreen vegetation and richly decorated with replicas of artworks discovered in the Villa dei Papiri, all reflecting the wealth, taste, and intellectual level of the erstwhile owners. But additionally, and important for our purposes, a recreated kitchen garden sits beside the Malibu Villa and provides a glimpse into the daily life of those long-vanished residents.

From written documents as well as the many surviving Roman murals in the imperial villas at Rome and especially in Pompeii it is possible to identify actual plants and reconfigure the distribution of trees, shrubs, and flowers, and the appearance of fences or walls. With their realistic pleasure garden scenes these murals were dedicated to the theme of the garden. Ivy (*Hedera helix*), evergreens, and acanthus (*Acanthus* spp.) formed the backdrop for box (*Buxus sempervirens*), myrtle (*Myrtus communis*), bay laurel (*Laurus nobilis*), oleander (*Nerium oleander*), pomegranate (*Punica granatum*), and the strawberry tree (*Arbutus unedo*); depicted, as well, were the blossoms of violet (*Viola odorata*), French rose (*Rosa gallica*), orrisroot (iris, *Iris × germanica* var. *florentina*), bindweed (*Convolvulus humilis*), poppy (*Papaver* spp.), daisy (*Bellis perennis*), and Madonna Lily (*Lilium candidum*).

Reconstruction of ancient herb and vegetable beds, however, is another matter and relies exclusively on literary sources because they were not pictured in any of the murals that have surfaced to date. The many Roman texts on the subjects of agriculture and gardening describe which plants were raised in vegetable gardens, either as foodstuffs or to flavor food, to decorate portraits of the gods, to delight guests, fill living areas with fragrance, or feed bees—but above all to ensure residents of the estate a supply of medicines. Yet these plants, which truly gave life to the inhabitants of the villas, left only rare traces and for a long time received no attention from the excavators of the ruined cities.

A name that will turn up with special frequency in the following pages is that of the Roman Pliny the Elder, who died in the eruption of Vesuvius in the year A.D. 79 and is thus so closely linked with the fate of the cities buried by Vesuvius. Of his thirty-seven-volume *Natural History*, sixteen report on plants, their history, and their use. Although not preserved in the original, his work was copied many times by monks in the medieval cloisters of Europe who transcribed and commented on the classical agricultural texts.

Many of Pliny's plant names were adopted by the Swedish botanist Carolus Linnaeus in 1735 when he systematized the designations of plants, which until then had varied widely from region to region. More recent scientific discoveries continue to correct the Linnaean taxonomy, which is identified by the presence of the initial L.; the corrections or revisions contain the name of the more recent botanists.

The illustrations of the plants described in the following pages date from the early nineteenth century, as few ancient depictions of them are extant. The earliest surviving illustrations of herbs are from the fifth century A.D., but they are not always clearly recognizable, and, as has been said, the murals found in Pompeiian and Herculanean houses show only pleasure gardens filled with trees, shrubs, and flowers, not the plants cultivated in kitchen gardens.

The herbs and vegetables grown in Roman gardens originated for the most part in the Mediterranean region, where some were still fairly new to domestication. However, few of the plants from the Villa in Malibu described in this work are native to North America. All the others were brought here in the course of the modern era by European explorers and settlers. Conversely, many plants that are widely thought to belong to Mediterranean flora, such as the sunflower (*Helianthus annuus*) and tomato (*Lycopersicon esculentum*), came from North or South America and did not reach the Old World until the seventeenth century; these, of course, are not included in this volume.

The Sources

Our notions of what Roman herb and vegetable gardens looked like and the uses of the plants derive primarily from the surviving texts of ancient authors who dealt with horticultural and agricultural subject matter, as already mentioned. Roman statesman Cato the Censor (234–149 B.C.) initiated this type of literature with his work *De agricultura (On agriculture)*. In what became something of a household diary, he reported his experiences as a landowner and planned to hand the texts down to his son and heirs as well as leave a record for the Roman government. In ancient Rome such agricultural heritage was bequeathed from father to son in the form of sayings like, "When the pear trees blossom, make a sacrifice for your cattle and begin spring plowing" (Cato *On agriculture* 131). Like all of the subsequent authors who dealt with the subject of gardening and agriculture, Cato drew on Greek works—especially the writings of a pupil of

Aristotle, Theophrastos (ca. 372–ca. 287 B.C.), who supplied for the first time fairly exact botanical and morphological descriptions of the plant world.

Marcus Terentius Varro (116–27 B.C.) was another member of the Roman aristocracy who, in addition to his political activity, also published a work on farming. His writing is especially noted for its wealth of quotations from older, lost Greek and Punic texts on the subject. Through his participation in Roman army campaigns, Varro amassed a considerable fortune that enabled him to assemble one of the largest libraries of his time. His work *De re rustica* (*On agriculture*) is a textbook in the form of a dialogue in which he refers to his own experience, like Cato before him. He established a calendar for planting in the garden and in the fields and quoted the oral tradition of his day in the vernacular of the farm populace.

Because of the great interest in the cultivation and use of plants, the works of these two Romans, along with that of Columella, were preserved in medieval manuscript collections produced in monastery scriptoria in the ninth or tenth century. Lucius Junius Moderatus Columella was born in the western part of the Roman Empire (Spain) in the first century A.D. He acquired several properties in the vicinity of imperial Rome and reported extensively on their management. A cultivated pragmatist, he boldly published a fine poem on gardening in which he refers to the verses of the Roman poet Virgil— whose poetic depictions of garden scenes convey some sense of the Romans' appreciation of nature and love for plants and their simple beauty. Columella can be relied upon for very precise descriptions and methods of horticultural practices.

While the authors cited above describe the practical experiences of very wealthy landowners, three other poets were proprietors of smaller estates where they, too, gained practical experience in gardening: Virgil (70–19 B.C.); Horace (65–8 B.C.); and Martial (A.D. 38/41–101/104). By referring to the verses and epigrams of these three, one can gain a sense of the significance of the garden in Roman daily life, as well as the Roman religious sensibility. For instance, in *Georgics* (songs about life on a farm), Virgil praises country life for the opportunity it affords one to observe the cycle of nature and vegetation's inexhaustible power of renewal. Just how much a small farmer's household garden meant to him is shown in the *Moretum* (Latin, meaning the plowman's lunch), a

highly atmospheric poem that is part of the *Appendix Vergiliana*, a collection of poems gathered in the Renaissance and attributed to Virgil. Realistically and in detail, the work reports on how a day laborer provided for himself from the produce of his garden and earned additional income by selling his surplus.

One of the most important sources, however, as noted previously, is the *Naturalis historia* (*Natural History*) of Gaius Plinius Secundus, or Pliny the Elder (23/24–79 A.D.), a native of Como raised in Rome, who perished beside the Gulf of Naples the day after the eruption of Vesuvius. His activity as an officer in the Roman army took him to the Roman provinces of northern and western Europe, where he eagerly studied local gardening methods and observed the influence of Roman horticulture. He is quoted frequently throughout the entries in this volume and therefore is referred to simply as Pliny.

The eastern part of the Roman Empire also figures prominently in our understanding of Roman gardening. Pedanius Dioscorides, a native of Anazarbus in Asia Minor (present-day Turkey), traveled widely in Greece and the eastern Mediterranean in the first century A.D. He is considered antiquity's most famous pharmacologist. His *Materia medica* (*Materials of medicine*) deals with the use of plants as foods and medicines from a medical standpoint and documents the full scope of knowledge at that time regarding the effects and uses of herbs and medicinal plants. Written in Greek, the medical teachings of Dioscorides appeared in Asia Minor just as Pliny's work on natural history was being composed in Rome to the west, though the two authors knew nothing of one another; they apparently, however, drew upon the same works of reference.

The major source on the role of plants in Roman- and Greek-influenced mythology was the *Metamorphoses* of Ovid (43 B.C.–A.D. 17). One of the best-known Roman poets, he visited Greece and Asia Minor on study tours and also described many Roman holidays in *Fasti* (*Calendar of feast days*). Dedicated to the emperor Augustus, the work remained unfinished, and only the holidays between January and June survive. The descriptions report on these holidays' origins and mythological significance, and on the plants that figured in the religious rites. Centuries later in Berlin in 1791, the antiquarian

Karl Philipp Moritz compiled information on all the known holidays of the ancient Romans and presented them in the first volume of his work on the antiquities of Rome, "Sacred Customs of the Romans" (*Anthousa, Die heiligen Gebräuche der Römer*), which completed modern understanding of the Romans' annual festival cycle.

In addition to the literature, works of natural history, and books on pharmacology, another major source on the use of plants was the so-called *Cookbook of Apicius*, which originated in the first century A.D. as well. The connoisseur Marcus Gavius Apicius, who took his own life upon discovering that his wealth no longer sufficed to keep him in the luxury he had known, reportedly left behind two books of recipes, which were expanded and completed in fourth-century editions under the title *De re coquinaria* (*On the art of cooking*). Many of his recipes are referred to in the entries below and provide a good idea of the elaborate range of Roman gastronomy.

Additional information on Roman gardens comes from the archaeological record. By burying Pompeii and Herculaneum, as well as the many luxurious villas in their vicinity, the catastrophic eruption of Vesuvius in A.D. 79 preserved traces of everyday life of the time on a scale seen nowhere else. However, excavations using modern methods were not undertaken at these locations until recent decades. Precise investigations have allowed us to study the architecture of Roman houses and also the multiple forms of contemporary gardens. Thanks in particular to the research and excavation carried out by Wilhelmina Jashemski, we now understand the appearance and significance of gardens in the everyday life of these Roman residents. Despite all literary efforts to describe the gardens, only an excavation can make clear how they actually looked in antiquity and how pleasure and food-producing gardens coexisted in close quarters within city walls. Small craftsmen's houses, rich urban villas, temples, sports facilities, cafes, and schools all had their gardens. However, Dr. Jashemski has also been able to identify flower and vegetable gardens, and vineyard patterns. The discovery of intersecting pathways in vineyards and the layout of beds in kitchen gardens, moreover, shows just how precise the descriptions were in the agrarian literature of the time. Because Roman murals depicted only refined pleasure gardens to the exclusion of utility plantings, we remain primarily dependent on the aforementioned literary sources to gain a sense of the appearance of kitchen gardens.

The Roman Vegetable Garden

The lives of Romans in a sense revolved around their kitchen gardens, which produced herbs for seasoning, salads and vegetables for daily meals, healing plants to relieve pain and cure illness, and flowers to decorate images of the gods. According to Pliny, gardening—which even the earliest Roman kings had practiced with their own hand (Pliny, *Natural History* 19.19)—was worthy of description because nothing had been as much admired as gardens since time immemorial. He mentioned both the mythical garden of the Hesperides in the west and the orchard of Helios (the sun god) in the east, as well as one described by Homer, the garden of Alkinoos, king of the Phaoacians, who later appeared in the works of Virgil. All these gardens were described as continuously fertile paradises—just what everyone wants in a garden.

In the twelve tables of Roman law, composed as early as the fifth century A.D., the garden is called *heredium* (legacy), while the country estate is not referred to as *villa* but simply as *hortus* (garden). In his treatise on farming Cato used the same term *hortus* for the irrigated vegetable garden, as Columella and Pliny (*Natural History* 19.19) would do somewhat later.

Cato warned anyone purchasing a country estate to pay attention to two things: the quality of its vineyards and the site of the kitchen garden, which requires healthy soil and access to water.

Gardens were frequently bounded by a wall, a fence, or a hedge, which served to reinforce the notion that the garden was an artificial, manmade construction that must be set off from untamed nature on every side. This separation is clearly implied in the

Indo-Germanic root *ghordo*, source of Greek *chortos*, Latin *hortus*, and English *garden*. Even the Persian *pairidaeʒa* (paradise) is originally just a word for demarcation and walling, fence, or hurdle.

"There is no doubt that a garden must adjoin the house, in such a way that it can be watered," Pliny advised, adding that the earth should be broken when the western winds start to blow, in the middle of February. The soil "should be mixed with manure and then divided up into beds. Each bed should be surrounded by an irrigation channel and a narrow path allowing one to approach" (Pliny *Natural History* 19.20).

As described in the following pages of his book, the desired plants are then set into each of these small plots. A myrtle tree (*Myrtus communis*) and a bay laurel (*Laurus nobilis*) were part of the permanent stand of the kitchen garden; their berries and leaves were popular seasonings, and their branches provided essential material for making fine wreaths. One corner of the garden housed the beehives, for sugar was unknown at the time and the sweetness of honey was widely sought after as both a delicacy and a preservative. As Cato had long since advised, flowers and garland materials were planted between the herbs and vegetables, a tradition that continued in the monastic gardens of the Middle Ages and even later.

A housewife or female overseer was responsible for the garden and its health. She had to take to heart Cato's warning: "In gardening you must do nothing too late, for delays can never be made up" (Cato *On agriculture* 5). Pliny remarked that at the sight of any shoddy garden one could immediately conclude that a lazy mistress was in charge (Pliny *Natural History* 19.19).

Moretum, Virgil's poem mentioned above, offers a vivid impression of the simple farmer's garden during the Roman imperial period. It tells of a small-scale farmer who goes at dawn to fetch foodstuffs from his garden for his own needs, but tries to leave something to sell. His garden is described as follows:

> Next to the little house stood the garden, shielded
> By light-netted fence and waving green seeds,
> Small in space, yet rich in varied herbs
> It contained everything that a poor man needs,
> And sometimes a wealthy neighbor would ask
> for some of his stock.
>
> (Virgil *Moretum* 60–64)

As is common in all rural societies, the Romans were inclined toward self-sufficiency. Wealthy landowners of the early imperial period—even the epicure Lucullus Licinius (ca. 117–58/56 B.C.), the Roman general—were no exception. At the most luxurious dinners Romans were proud to serve products from their own land.

The Use of Plants

The importance of garden plants to the Romans is inescapable: Plants were essential nutritionally, medicinally, aromatically, cosmetically, and religiously.

To underline the importance of garden plants as nutrition, the authors in antiquity always cited the argument that the smartest animals were those that fed only on fruits and herbs. We must therefore pay more heed to the plants in the garden, Pliny urged, and, small and inexpensive though they be, we have to honor and value them all the more. Evidently, Pliny thought his contemporary Romans needed to be reminded of the value of garden plants' simpler uses.

Many plants, such as chicory (*Cichorium intybus*), fennel (*Foeniculum vulgare*) and lovage (*Levisticum officinale*), were consumed raw as salads. For Pliny these uncooked foods provided a useful reminder of the virtues and eating habits of old Rome—and the occasion for warning his contemporaries against too much luxury. He described the virtue of these raw foods as always handy and easy to prepare, easy to digest and not dulling to the senses; they save on fuel because they can be eaten raw, and reduce the need to import costly spices (*Natural History* 19.19).

Included in the entries that follow are ancient recipes for virtually all of the Malibu Villa's herbs. Nearly all the plants were used frequently as a food or at least as a seasoning in food, and served either at simple countryside meals or lavish banquets for wealthy and influential guests.

Plants were essential sources for foods, but equally essential for medicines. All of the entries describing these herbs from the Villa's garden include at least one and often several medicinal uses. Herbs were chopped, minced, ground, dried, mixed into liquids, or stirred into pastes; honey was the medium to make some palatable. For salves, plants such as chamomile (*Chamaemelum nobile*), orrisroot (iris, *Iris × germanica* var. *florentina*), sweet marjoram (*Origanum majorana*), French rose (*Rosa gallica*), and spearmint (*Mentha spicata*) were used. Tinctures were concocted from hollyhock (*Alcea rosea*), yellow sweet clover (*Melilotus officinalis*), and rue (*Ruta graveolens*). Pliny greatly admired the skills of his Mediterranean ancestors for their inventive applications of herbs as medicines:

Observing the famous herbs that our earth-mother Tellus produces just for medicines fills me with admiration for the good sense of our fathers, who left nothing unexplored, nothing untried, and thus discovered things that benefit their descendants.

(Pliny *Natural History* 25.1)

Full of pride, Pliny quoted claims by the Greek plant experts that the most powerful herbs grew in Italy. With advice that might sound familiar today, he tried to convince his contemporaries to take their health seriously and return to using the plants in their gardens. Never have we loved life more, Pliny wrote, yet never have we cared so little about sustaining that love. Delicacies and luxury make life more delicious to us, but who honors the herbs that serve to drive out pain and to stave off death? We consider concern for our health someone else's business and hope that doctors will be good enough to relieve us of the chore (*Natural History* 22.7).

The myriad uses of herbs as essential medicines are described in greater detail in the entries. However, the cosmetic and aromatic uses of herbs were also of great importance to the Romans, and many herbs were the source of fragrances to perfume places and people. Wafting herbal scents were often part of rituals performed during the worship of the gods—scents from particular plants believed to be sacred to a god. The fragrant air resulted from burning branches or twigs of herbs or scattering strongly aromatic leaves, flowers, or twigs about an altar or a temple site—or a domestic room. In antiquity foul odors were not uncommon due to perishable foods, wine, sickness, and death. To have a fresh, pleasant aroma to counter the malodorous was both desirable

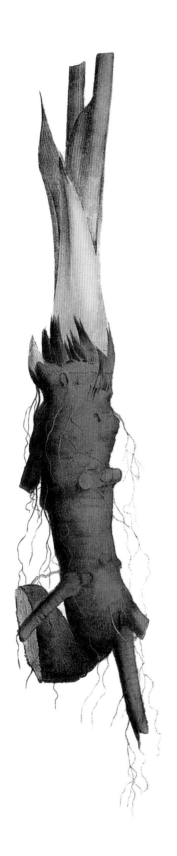

and often necessary. Among others, the herbs used for this purpose were orrisroot (iris, *Iris × germanica* var. *florentina*), French rose (*Rosa gallica*), chamomile (*Chamaemelum nobile*), sweet marjoram (*Origanum marjorana*), sweet yellow clover (*Melilotus officinalis*), and spearmint (*Mentha spicata*). It is hardly surprising that the oils of certain of these same herbs became the perfumes that scented the bodies of the ancient Romans, particularly the iris and French rose just mentioned. Crowns woven from whole plants provided the same effect.

The interrelationship between religion and nature for the Romans is clear from the numerous altars discovered in gardens, fields, and sacred groves. Since earliest times the Romans sacrificed out of doors to a range of divinities, offering all manner of gifts in recognition of the gifts they themselves received from nature. The Romans, like all people, were dependent upon nature, and thus plants had significant religious meaning for them. Nature and the gods provided their food and medicine, and the gods shielded them—or didn't—from catastrophes such as poor harvests, famine, or flood. At the many altars, grateful Romans made offerings of oil and wine, fruits, herbs, and flowers as well as various sacrificial animals. Often sacred branches or garlands were placed on the altar before a sacrifice. Holidays were celebrated throughout the year for the purpose of seeking certain gods' blessings of undertakings such as the sowing of seed, the seed itself, of blossoms, of plants' growth, and especially of the final harvest. Related to the cycles of nature, these holiday celebrations were expressions of respect and gratitude for nature's gifts and included festive public and private rites and sacrificial meals.

Garden Celebrations

The celebratory cycle began in January. If the farmer had been successful, he thanked Tellus (goddess of earth) by offering her a well-fed sow. Next, after the successful germination of his seeds and his plants' growth he would thank Ceres. The Romans believed she was the goddess who had first taught humans the art of plowing and the deliberate cultivation of plants for food. Ceres could likewise ensure fertility and plentiful yield, as could her Roman sister-goddesses of flowers and fruit, Flora and Pomona: Each had their own rites and priests with costly vestments and easily identifiable attributes.

By the seventeenth of March when the grapes began to grow, Liberalia was celebrated in honor of Bacchus, originally called Liber Pater, whom the Romans believed made men glad and freed them from all care. For a time, another springtime ritual

honored the god Robigus on the twenty-fifth of April. Although he and the celebration fell into oblivion, he had the rather important duty of protecting grain from wheat rust.

April, however, was truly dedicated to Venus (the Greeks' Aphrodite), who was associated with gardens and whose festival ushered in the month. This goddess of enduring importance grew to be equal to Jupiter (Greek, Zeus) in the Romans' view, which was remarkable: Jupiter was lord of the heavens, god of weather, the state, its laws, and its welfare. In the early stages of the complex Roman belief system, Venus seems to have been the goddess of newly sprouted seed—growth and fertility. She became, however, the link between the gods in their heaven and humans on earth: She accompanied humans to Elysium. Venus was believed to be the foremost protector of all gardens, no matter whether a pleasure or a kitchen garden.

The month of April ended with a feast for Flora, who showered all Italy with her abundance at this season. The Floralia, the name for the feast between the twenty-eighth of April and the third of May, and known since 240 B.C., were among the most conspicuously joyful of the Roman calendar: Every house was decked, every table was strewn, every person was crowned with flowers, and songs were sung to honor the blossoming world. On the first of May crowns of flowers decorated the hearths of homes, and smaller crowns were placed on the statuettes of the Lares, the protective gods of hearth and home.

Nature flourished over the summer months, and by August the celebrations would commence again. The grape harvest began at the end of August, and thus on the twenty-first of the month the Romans feasted in honor of Bacchus and Venus. A small garden altar in Pompeii was even dedicated to these two plus another god—Hercules (the Greek Herakles). He was honored in gardens in the hope that he might grant unending fertility due to his association with the mythic garden of the Hesperides and its golden apples.

No Greek roots existed for Pomona, a goddess only for the Etruscans and Romans, but the Romans believed she was the guardian of fruits, particularly those from orchards. During the late summer season prayers for her blessings and a rich harvest were accompanied by fruit offerings on altars in her sanctuaries. Her fruits were thought to be the first foods of humans. Accordingly, Pomona was thought to be in conflict with Ceres, goddess of the fruits and herbs of the fields. Fruit from trees grew closer to heaven than the fruits of the fields—orchard fruit even caused one to glance heavenward—thus the healing powers and significance of tree fruits should be greater, or so the argument ran.

Diana, the moon goddess, was also honored in ancient villa gardens, where sweet-smelling herbs and resins were burned before her statues. She was considered a guardian of fruits and vegetables, too. Sometimes identified with the Roman goddess Luna (Latin, moon), Diana was the purveyor of night's moisture and coolness and was equally important for the success of the garden as was her brother Apollo, who provided the natural world with the life-giving force of sunlight. Apollo, god of solar light, was closely identified with the Roman god of the sun, Sol (Latin, sun).

On the thirteenth of October crowns were fashioned with leaves and flowers from gardens and used in the feast of Fontinalia, when they were thrown

into wells and springs to bless water, the other crucial element for a successful garden.

Although not associated with a particular holiday or feast, a Roman garden would hardly fail to have a statue of Priapus. This curious being, adopted from eastern religions, possessed a grossly oversized phallus that symbolized the fertility of all the surrounding vegetation. Scarecrow-like, he was intended to frighten and drive out thieves and animals. A magic talisman against all evil-doers, he might be fashioned from the wood of a fig tree or, less commonly, take the form of a precious bronze herm, as can be seen today at the Villa in Malibu. Pliny counted statues of Priapus among the *satyrica signa* (satyr-like signs), a tradition from which he traced the custom of decorating gardens with works of art. "We can see," wrote Pliny, "that a certain superstition prevailed here, and that although gardens

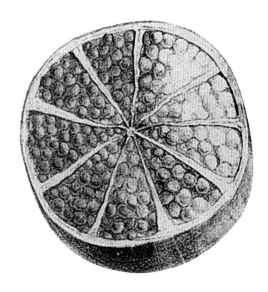

were under Venus's protection, satyr-like signs were erected there to ward off envy and evil spells" (Pliny *Natural History* 19.19).

The Significance of Plants in Religion and Mythology

Some herbs and flowers played an important role in Greek and Roman mythology. The story of the Greek goddess of love, Aphrodite, shows how interwoven Greek and Roman culture history is. The Greek figure of Aphrodite is merged with the Roman goddess of vegetation, Venus. Gods also suffer their fates, and thus we hear of Aphrodite falling in love with a mortal, the Trojan shepherd Anchises, to whom she bore a son, Aeneas. He became the mythical ancestor of the Latin tribe who finally landed on the coast of Italy after many battles and misfortunes. According to Virgil, the cherished Aeneas was wounded in one of these conflicts by a deadly arrow. His divine mother hastened to Crete, and there, near the birthplace of Zeus, plucked the herb Cretan dittany (*Origanum dictamnus*), which was the only one that could heal the wound. As early as 350 B.C., Aristotle had first reported on the healing power of Cretan dittany, and his pupil Theophrastos described it in his work on plants. About 29 B.C. the Roman poet Virgil associated the herb with Venus, and versions of the ancient story recur in modern times in the earliest printed herbals.

Roses and particularly myrtle (*Myrtus communis*) were considered sacred to Venus. Her images in temples were decked with myrtle and washed in a bath saturated with myrtle. Bacchus (the Greek Dionysos) was associated with the grape (*Vitis vinifera*) and ivy

(*Hedera helix*), which were believed to be sacred to him; grapes and ivy were his attributes in works of art.

The connection between the plant world and the sacred, as well as the blending of Roman and Greek religion and custom, is illustrated by the history of bay laurel (*Laurus nobilis*). This evergreen, aromatic tree, native to both Greece and Italy, saw great application. In archaic Rome, pairs of bay laurel trees were placed before the official sanctuaries of the oldest priests in order to create an especially sacred sphere, while crowns and branches of bay laurel were presented to victorious gladiators. An earlier story from Greece told how Apollo, god of light, whose name remained unchanged from the Greek, slew a dragon and then cleansed himself with bay laurel branches. This story, like the metamorphosis of the nymph Daphne, reportedly took place in the Vale of Tempe in northern Greece, an important destination during the Roman imperial period. For the Romans, the place represented the ideal mythical landscape with its contrasting steep mountain cliffs and gentle meadow bottoms fragrant with bay laurel. The plant became symbolic of the beneficial gifts of Apollo in the Roman religious/mythological world view: The god cleansed and protected humans from all evil and imparted visionary gifts. The Pythia, who spoke the oracles of Apollo at Delphi, reportedly used the powers of bay laurel when uttering her wise pronouncements in Apollo's name. The god's mythical tripod in the temple at Delphi was decorated with bay laurel garlands, and victors in the arts competitions were crowned with its leafy branches. The emperor Augustus vowed to the god Apollo that he would erect a temple in his honor on the Palatine Hill in Rome. In accordance with an old Roman tradition bay

trees stood before Augustus's relatively modest home. The emperor's significance was reinforced through a very personal association with Apollo, who is said to have sent Augustus a bay laurel branch that flourished. The entry below for bay laurel expands on this myth.

Pomegranate (*Punica granatum*) and spearmint (*Mentha spicata*) are associated with the outcome in the struggle between Pluto (the Greek Hades, god of the Underworld), and Ceres (Demeter), the great earth mother, as can be seen in the entries for spearmint, pomegranate, and opium poppy.

The Greek goddess Athena drove her spear into the rock of the Acropolis of Athens, and the weapon became an olive tree (*Olea europaea*), the sign of divine peace. This olive symbolized the sacred peace of Olympian Zeus, which was declared every four years for the duration of the games at Olympia. At these ancient sacred games victors were presented with crowns from the branches of wild olive trees. The branches were cut in the holy grove of the temple district with a golden knife and then woven into slender crowns. A herald proclaimed the victor's name, his father's name, and that of his home city, and a priest robed in purple placed the crown on the victor's head. One ancient source sarcastically reported that the champion would be dragged from one celebratory event to another, as might happen to a celebrated athlete today, and his olive crown would soon become as dried out as his glory. Whatever the outcome of the athlete's fame, the olive was of essential importance in both Italy and Greece, and remains so today. The entry below for celery documents the fact that other plants were considered sacred and used in other major cities for their victors' crowns during the four-year cycle of the games.

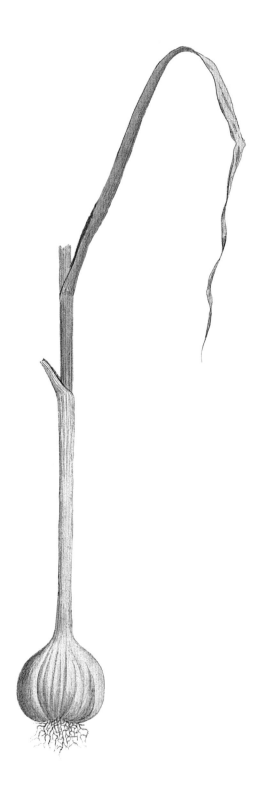

Herbs for the Kitchen

Through the excavations in Pompeii and Herculaneum, we get a good picture of the Roman kitchen, in which herbs, roots, fruits, lettuces, and vegetables from the adjacent kitchen garden were processed. In an average-size house, food was prepared in a fairly small room without windows. The kitchen would have an oven for baking bread and cakes, an open fireplace, and a water basin. The most important tools were knives; spoons made of wood, metal, and bone; mortars; bronze and ceramic saucepans; and skewers and spits for grilling meat.

Large amphorae contained wine, fermented fruit juice, oil, and the famous so-called *garum*, a sauce whose main ingredients were fish and herbs. It was bought ready-made and used for almost all dishes. This sauce was about as ubiquitous as soy sauce is in the modern Oriental kitchen. On the other hand, salt was not much used. Under the strict super-vision of the housewife, slaves were responsible for the cooking on the fire. Grand houses and villas with large kitchens employed well-paid cooks, while less wealthy households engaged a professional cook only for large parties and important occasions.

After an extensive breakfast, which included porridge and herbed cheese, and a small snack in the middle of the day, the evening meal after sunset was the high point of the day. Family and guests then gathered around a large table either indoors or in the garden, depending on the season.

The more elegant Roman evening meal consisted of three rounds of dishes. First came small appetizers, such as vegetables, salads, olives, mushrooms, oysters, egg dishes, or the very popular dormice. The second, or main course, consisted of various meat, game, or fish dishes, each accompanied by more or less sophisticated sauces. Sweets and fruits, or cheeses and sausages, finished off the meal.

Compared to today, Romans had only a small selection of hot and cold drinks. They were limited to goat or sheep's milk, wine, beer, water, and some herb teas. Wine was the most esteemed drink and was part of any important meal. A white wine sweetened with honey was served with the first course; for the main course there was wine mixed with water. Depending on the time of year, the wine could be infused with violets (*Viola odorata*), rose petals (*Rosa gallica*), or with the fragrant orrisroot (iris, *Iris × germanica* var. *florentina*). Wine was also seasoned with fennel seeds (*Foeniculum vulgare*) or cumin seeds (*Cuminum cyminum*). A sweet and heavy muscatel, made from late-harvest grapes, was usually served as a dessert.

In order to prolong the ample meal, the host might offer the herb-infused liqueur *oxygarum*, whose main ingredients were honey, vinegar, celery (*Apium graveolens*), parsley (*Petroselinum crispum*), caraway seed (*Carum carvi*), lovage (*Levisticum officinale*), and bay laurel (*Laurus nobilis*).

Oxyporum was very popular for weak stomachs and colics. This was a fermented drink made of common quince (*Cydonia oblonga*) or pomegranate (*Punica granatum*) mixed with vinegar, honey, caraway (*Carum carvi*), rue (*Ruta graveolens*), ginger (*Zingiber officinale*), and pepper (*Piper nigrum*). The farmer Columella's recommendation for the end of a meal was a drink called *glechonites*, made of wine, absinth or common wormwood (*Artemisia absinthium*), hyssop (*Hyssopus officinalis*), pennyroyal (*Mentha pulegium*), and thyme (*Thymus vulgaris*) (Columella *On Agriculture* 12.35).

Tomatoes (*Lycopersicon esculentum*), corn (*Zea mays*), and cocoa (*Theobroma cacao*)—all so important for Italian cooking today—were not known before the discovery of the Americas. The squash that was frequently used in the Roman kitchen was the bottle gourd (*Lagenaria siceraria*), which is indigenous to the Old World. All kinds of garden herbs were used in its preparation.

Roman eating habits had changed over time. Republican Rome was still sustained exclusively by homegrown products, as several sources mentioned above testify: Cato, Varro, Virgil, Horace, and Pliny all glorified life in ancient Rome. The writings of Martial, Petronius (d. A.D. 66), and Juvenal (A.D. 67–138) give insight into the eating habits and luxurious lives at the time of the Roman Empire, by which time herbs and roots from three continents—Africa, Asia, and Europe—were available kitchen ingredients.

Of the many ancient cookbooks, only the one by Apicius has survived. This gourmet is said to have left two books of recipes. The first, called *De condituris* (*On sauces*), dealt exclusively with a most refined area of cooking, the preparation of exquisite sauces. Fortunately, several of these recipes were later incorporated into his other cookbook, *De re coquinaria* (*On the art of cooking*). These recipes describe very clearly the many uses of fresh and dried herbs, vegetables, and fruits in the ancient Roman cuisine as cited in the following entries.

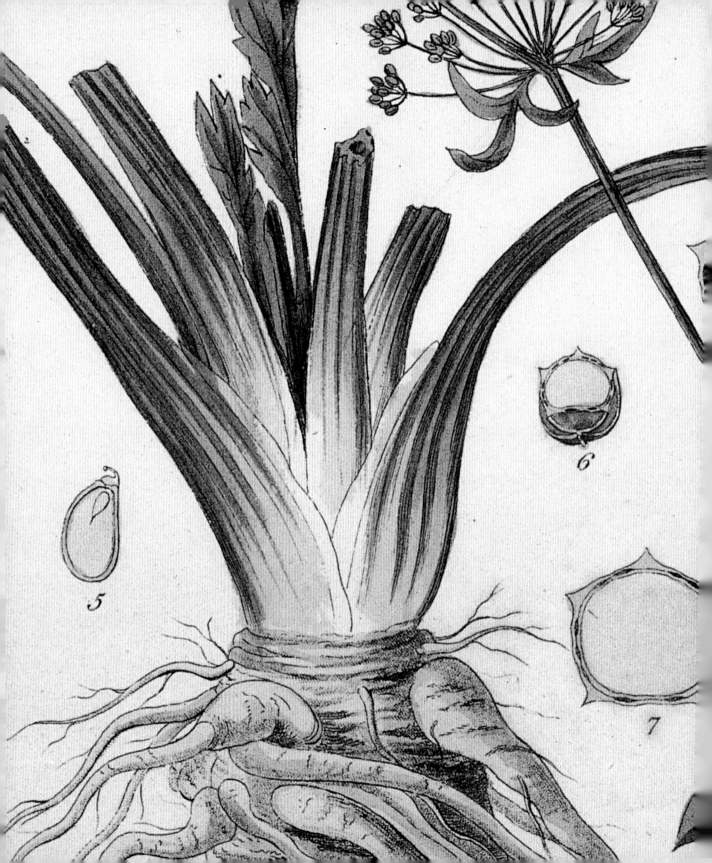

absinthe

Every ancient herb garden had to include this elegant, silver-gray shrub. By the first century B.C., the plant had become known as the "mother of herbs." It takes its Greek name from Artemisia, believed to be the protector of women and facilitator of labor; indeed, this herb was thought to soothe women in pain and assist them in childbirth—besides providing a convenient way out of an unwanted pregnancy. The Latin *absinthium* makes figurative reference to the plant as something bitter yet healthful.

Renowned for his gardens and their valuable descriptions, Pliny reported on an interesting Roman custom:

> Everyone agrees on the utility of wormwood, this plant that is easy to find and has more uses than nearly any other; it has become famous, moreover, in the festive holidays of the Roman people, because in the great festival of the Latins the four-horse chariots run races on the Capitoline Hill, and the victor receives a drink of wormwood. This is done, in my opinion, because our forefathers believed it a great honor to receive good health as your prize.
>
> (Pliny *Natural History* 27.28)

Even in antiquity, "wormwood drops" were proverbial for their bitter taste. Ancient verses depicted the way children were treated for stomach cramps with the beneficial but bitter plant: The rim of the glass or spoon with the medication was dipped in honey to deceive the unsuspecting youngster.

Pliny noted that the plant was easy to find beyond the confines of the garden. In fact, since prehistoric times *Artemisia absinthium*—native to Europe and Asia—cropped up around human settlements without any encouragement from cultivation. However, it was far simpler to have such an important medicinal plant within handy reach in your own herbal bed, where its many-branching leafy stalks could be easily harvested and dried in summer.

Pliny stated that the use of *Artemisia absinthium* prevented drunkenness after excessive wine consumption. The herb was thought to stimulate the appetite, promote digestion, suppress flatulence, alleviate headaches, and cure jaundice and epilepsy. But it was used for more than just medicine. Absinthe, or common wormwood, was a popular flavoring for wine, and a recipe mentioned in the cookbook of the gourmet Apicius for "Roman Absinthe" may be the original source for the famous Italian aperitif vermouth. If one mixed a bit of absinthe wine with one's ink, book scrolls could be protected from the insect damage of mites. Dried bouquets of the herb were deemed a remedy for one of the most plaguing problems of ancient daily life—moths that attacked winter woolens stored in trunks.

There were myriad reasons to reserve a corner in one's garden for this versatile plant!

COMMON WORMWOOD *Artemisia absinthium* (Asteraceae)
Nees van Esenbeck, no. 235

Absynthium officinale R.
Artemisia Absynthium. Lin.

anise

"In your home herb garden, be sure to plant anise in abundance." This advice was already hundreds of years old by Pliny's day, passed down orally from the Greek philosopher Pythagoras (ca. 580–ca. 500 B.C.), whose ideas were beginning to enjoy a certain vogue in Rome during the first century B.C. However, by citing such authority, Pliny no doubt hoped to emphasize the importance of anise, the herb he discussed more than any other. Pythagoras had reportedly extolled the use of the root, leaf, and seeds of anise and urged its consumption, both raw and cooked. He supposedly wrote that an epileptic who grasped anise in his hand need fear no further seizures. Women could expect the immediate easing of labor pains after just a whiff, and a puree of anise seeds cooked with milk and barley was guaranteed to restore a mother's strength after delivery. Indeed, travelers who drank an anise concoction would feel immediately refreshed and equal to any exertion.

On awakening in the morning, still fasting, you should mix anise seeds with a bit of honey, chew them, and rinse your mouth with wine— Pliny's recipe for irresistibly sweet-smelling breath (Pliny *Natural History* 20.72).

Anise seeds were also used extensively to flavor breads and sweet pastries. The green leaves were served as a vegetable or cooked in herbal soups. Juice extracted from the leaves was a popular digestive aid after heavy meals, and offered relief from nausea and vomiting. Insomniacs could anticipate a night's rest by sipping this beverage. However, the surest preventive for insomnia was to suspend a bunch of dried anise above the would-be sleeper's nose—the aroma did the trick. The root was once prized for its ability to aid the stomach and to combat spells of coughing or high fever.

Apicius, the Roman gastronome, left a delicious recipe for pork with anise, and he may have been among those who called anise the "unavoidable" herb. In those days of excess indulgence and frequent repletion—when, as Pliny had caustically remarked, Romans no longer grew hungry from their labors— it was anise, as appetizer, that restored the urge to eat yet again.

Native to the East, licorice-tasting anise is a very old cultivated plant. In Roman antiquity, anise from the isle of Crete was ranked the very finest, followed by the Egyptian variety. It is cultivated today in a great many regions and it is also widely available in the wild state. It can be quite a finicky plant, and prefers poor, light, well-drained soil.

Anise *Pimpinella anisum* (Apiaceae)
Nees van Esenbeck, no. 275

Pimpinella Anisum Lin.

asafetida

Ferula assa-foetida, with its peculiar name and less than agreeable fragrance, originated in Persia and Afghanistan and became known in the Mediterranean basin after the campaigns of Alexander the Great (d. 323 B.C.). Grown since then as a luxuriant shrub with comely, umbrella-like yellow blossoms, it was valued in antiquity mostly as a substitute for the much-prized miracle plant *Ferula silphium*, which grew exclusively in the vicinity of Cyrene in Libya. All attempts to naturalize this coveted plant in Greece and Italy failed, and due to intensive exploitation it was nearly extinct by the first century A.D.

The stalk and root of *Ferula silphium* secrete a resinous liquid that in minute amounts gives food a refined spiciness. It was the first exotic spice to enrich Roman cuisine. So expensive was this herb that the connoisseur Apicius gave his wealthy readers a tip on how to stretch their supply by placing some of it in a fine glass vessel with twenty pine nuts, and using only a small amount of the nuts when its flavor was needed.

The Greek Theophrastos left a description of *Ferula silphium* that corresponds closely with images of the plant on ancient silver coins minted in Cyrene beginning ca. 530 B.C. The coin depicts the spice because its export figured prominently in the country's economy. It shows the not-yet sprouted plant, whose stalk is sheathed, onionlike, by the juicy lower leaves and it was consumed at this stage as a prized fresh vegetable. But the most precious product was the rubbery resin secreted from the stalk or root at the slightest abrasion.

Resin can also be extracted from the related, still-extant *Ferula assa-foetida*. Despite the change of name and provenance, its resin has been used over the centuries as a spice and medicine. According to the Greek pharmacologist Dioscorides, its juice, mixed with honey, was applied to the eyes as a remedy for cataracts and declining visual acuity. Sufferers from toothache were advised to insert a little of the viscous liquid into the offending tooth or use it, diluted with vinegar and water, as a mouthwash.

Romans of Apicius's day may have used remnants of the then rare *Ferula silphium* (known as *laserpicium*). However, they had begun to replace it with resin extracted from asafoetida because it was a highly desired flavoring for the most exotic of dishes —roast flamingo, the then quite rare guinea fowl, or stuffed dormouse!

ASAFETIDA *Ferula assa-foetida* (Apiaceae)
Nees van Esenbeck, no. 293

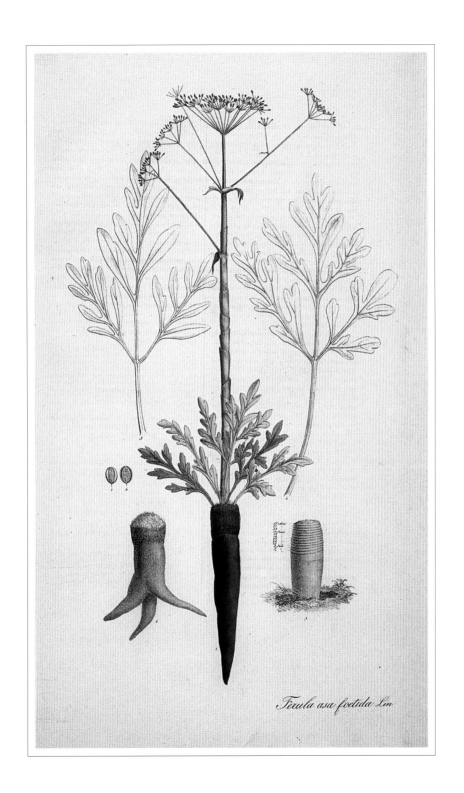

Ferula asa fœtida Lin.

basil

Modern Italian cuisine would be unthinkable without it, and yet in the ancient cookbook by Apicius, basil makes just one appearance—as an ingredient in a fresh herbal sauce, where it was added to a dish of chopped leeks, braised in olive oil, with caraway seed and coriander, and mixed with young peas. The vinaigrette sauce was made from wine, *garum* (a popular Roman condiment), pepper, and basil.

Aromatic basil, native to India where it was revered, probably became known in Greece following the campaigns of Alexander the Great in the fourth century B.C. Its intense fragrance inspired Theophrastos to call it *ocimum*, a term derived from the words for "smell" and "sharp." *Basilicum* (Greek, meaning "royal") must have been added later, since the ancient Greeks had little affection for basil and would scarcely have called it royal.

The Greek pharmacologist Dioscorides considered basil hard to digest, although he recommended a juice produced from its seeds as a remedy for melancholy. He cautioned, however, that sniffing the seeds or leaves could bring on a powerful sneezing fit. Physicians from Hippocrates' circle (ca. 460–ca. 377 B.C.), on the other hand, did prescribe basil for diarrhea and nausea.

Pliny attempted to refute his predecessors' superstitious belief that basil caused insanity or liver ailments. His experience showed that the scent of basil relieved fainting spells, excessive drowsiness, and headaches—the sufferer had only to apply a compress moistened with a mixture of basil leaves and vinegar or rose oil.

Cooked in wine, basil reduced flatulence, eased painful belching, and proved effective with stomach colic, all fitting benefits from a member of the mint family.

In the Roman herb garden, basil was a welcomed plant. According to Columella, "basil remains, just as it was sown, in its place and demands no more care than to be fertilized and weeded. It can be sown in fall or spring" (Columella *On Agriculture* 11.3). He liked using the herb to flavor olives for his table. One further note on basil's care in the garden is from Pliny, who said that the plant should be watered only at midday.

COMMON or SWEET BASIL *Ocimum basilicum* (Lamiaceae)
Nees van Esenbeck, no. 184

184.

Ocÿmum Basilicum

bay laurel

Every educated Roman knew the Greek legend of Daphne, who was transformed into a bay laurel tree to escape Apollo's pursuit. The evergreen bay, native to Greece and Italy, was a sacred plant in the sanctuary at Delphi, dedicated to Apollo, god of healing. Bay was therefore relied upon to protect against all evil. Only the god himself and the victors in the festival games in his honor were allowed to be crowned with bay laurel; a crown of this plant was not the customary sign of victory and peace until the Roman period.

Whenever the Romans got word of a victory, they suspended crowns and sprigs of bay laurel over their front doors. The same was done at the feast of the new year, for the plant brought luck and dispelled the evil spirits believed to lurk about a home's entrance for a chance to get inside. By the reign of Caesar Augustus, the custom was revived of placing two potted bay trees before the house of the Roman high priest. The pair of bay laurels was believed to be especially sacred—a belief with some merit when one considers a long-lived legend: One day an eagle flying overhead dropped the sprig of bay it was bearing into the lap of the emperor's wife, Livia. She planted the sprig in the earth, where it prodigiously yielded sacred trees sufficient to provide triumphal crowns for Augustus and all his successors.

Pliny claimed that bay laurel was the only tree never struck by lightning. Apparently, Emperor Tiberius always wore a bay crown when a thunderstorm broke over Rome.

Aromatic bay laurel suited one Roman ideal—a garden plant that was as useful as it was beautiful. In the pleasure gardens of Roman villas, people enjoyed strolling in the cooling shade of bay laurel's evergreen leaves. As described by Pliny the Younger (A.D. 61/62–113, nephew of the natural historian Pliny), the bay grew behind low box hedges (*Buxus sempervirens*) and threw shadows that merged with those of the taller plane trees (*Platanus* spp.).

Bay laurel was grown in vegetable gardens to provide flavoring for roasts. It medicated shortness of breath or headache and provided material for the prized crowns and woven front-door garlands. Most prized of all was the oil produced from the berries and leaves, which could banish exhaustion and grant dependable relief from neuralgia, ear problems, and influenza. For uterine problems or bladder inflammation ancient physicians recommended sitting baths infused with the boiled leaves of bay laurel; an extract from the berries was believed to be most effective for problems with the liver or kidneys.

Bay laurel was popular for smoking in both sacred and profane contexts.

BAY, SWEET BAY *Laurus nobilis* (Lauraceae)
Nees van Esenbeck, no. 132

Laurus nobilis

bee balm

Bee balm, or bee leaf as it was known in the ancient world, was named from the Greek word *melissa*, which originally referred only to the honey bee, but came to designate this herb so attractive to bees.

No farmer, said Columella, was likely to quibble about bee balm's mythic origin—as a beautiful woman whom Jupiter (Zeus) transformed into a honey bee. What mattered on the farm was to have bee balm around your hives for healthy bees and quality honey. Columella said that no one wrote more artfully about bee cultivation than Virgil (in *Georgics*, first century B.C.). Columella quoted the poet's instructions to collect bee balm early in spring and "press the bee balm leaf" and forcefully rub the extract on beehives to saturate them with the juice's aroma. Pliny also offered advice on this matter and explained that if beehives or bee houses were well coated with bee balm leaves, bees would not abandon them, for bees favored this blossom more than any other and were observed to disperse more slowly where it grew in profusion. The nectar from the flower was, of course, the primary attraction for the honey bees.

Bee balm, however, benefited humans in ways other than honey production. It was used as a medicinal plant as well as a delicate spice, and thus it was planted in domestic herb gardens as well as the areas surrounding hives. Bee balm's delicate leaves taste best and have the strongest effect when harvested shortly before they blossom. The ancients believed the leaves quickly helped treat stings from bees, hornets, or wasps. A mixture of the leaves with saltpeter and wine promised relief from stomachaches, inflammations, boils, gout, and dysentery. Extensively, eye irritations were treated with a juice from bee balm leaves and honey. The attractively jagged leaves were even used for personal ornamentation when bound together to make herbal wreaths.

Much of these uses are current today, since bee balm's antispasmodic and soothing properties are used for abdominal pain, and its antibacterial agents have a positive effect on inflammations and sores.

From its home in the East, bee balm was cultivated early in the Mediterranean region, where it also grew wild. Later it was cultivated elsewhere in Europe, in temperate Asia, and in North America, and it spread beyond the garden wall as well. Its plants have astonishing longevity and reach ages of up to thirty years. *Melissa officinalis* should not be confused with North America's native *Monarda didyma* (also called bee balm), which did not reach Europe until the eighteenth century.

LEMON BALM, SWEET MARY *Melissa officinalis* (Lamiaceae)
Nees van Esenbeck, no. 180

Melissa officinalis.

caraway

Caraway is a familiar little seed that does the stomach good and tastes most agreeably, according to the Greek Dioscorides, a native of Asia Minor (present-day Turkey). According to his Roman contemporary Pliny, that region was also the home of caraway. Pliny classified it as a foreign plant and referred to it by its ancient Latin name after the region of Caria in Asia Minor. Apparently he was unaware that caraway is also native to northern Italy.

In any case, the caraway family includes twenty-five varieties that are found in Europe, North Africa, nontropical Asia, and North America, where Native Americans, like the inhabitants of ancient and present-day Italy, used it as a spice and to quiet crying children.

The flavorful herb was brought from field to garden, where the carrotlike roots grew into large, tasty specimens in good soil without much moisture. Similar to the root of wild parsnip, caraway root was a popular vegetable, as Dioscorides mentions in his description. The young leaves were prepared like spinach or mixed with other greens to make spring-time soups. Caraway blossoms are so popular with bees that it made good sense to grow the plant in the garden since honey was very important for the house-hold in antiquity. But the highly valued seeds inspired the cultivation and harvesting of caraway because Roman connoisseurs would not do without the popular spice, considering it second only to cumin.

Apicius's cookbook abounds in refined recipes in which the two herbs, caraway and cumin, agreeably complement one another. Combined, they set off to perfection a dish of chicken with squash (*Lagenaria siceraria*), accompanied by a sauce of peaches, dates, truffles and herbs, olive oil, wine, honey, and vinegar. In another recipe, cumin lends peas their tanginess, while in the accompanying sauce caraway sets up the flavor of fresh basil—the unique use of basil in currently documented Roman cooking.

Dioscorides knew of caraway's digestive bene-fits; he understood that its essential oil stimulated secretion of gastric juices and acted antispasmodically on the stomach and intestines. Blood circulation could be stimulated by caraway, and it was thought helpful for rheumatic ailments. Ingesting caraway might encourage the production of breast milk, just as it could soothe digestive disorders in small children. These applications appear to have been common in both the ancient Old World and in North America, as suggested above by the use of the herb to calm small children.

CARAWAY *Carum carvi* (Apiaceae)
Nees van Esenbeck, no. 276

Carum Carvi Lin.

celery

Romans had a great fondness for celery and used its leaves and seeds for three foods that were required daily fare. Celery was an essential flavoring for daily bread, for curing green olives—both basic foodstuffs—and for the popular herb cheese *moretum*. Virgil's poem *Moretum* describes the daily activities of a humble farmer, including his preparation of the herb cheese, for which he plucked celery's decorative leaves.

But the more refined Roman cuisine also required celery: It was used in the digestive drink *oxygarum* and to complete *garum*, a very popular, widely used condiment. Although an essential ingredient in foods, celery appeared no less often as a remedy for stomach, intestinal, or kidney ailments. Celery was in the concoction called *theriac*, which was used to cure all manner of poisons: This mixture of opium and herbs, invented by the emperor Nero's physician Andromachos, was by medieval times thought to cure every kind of illness.

No other plant figured as prominently as celery in the earliest medicinal writings from ancient Egypt; however, celery was important for more than its medicinal properties. Eighteenth-century-B.C. specimens of Egyptian floral decoration clearly demonstrate its ornamental use. This traditional use continued in Greece and Rome, where celery-leaf crowns were mentioned with some frequency in connection with the popular symposia or banquets. The renowned sixth-century-B.C. Greek poet and singer Anacreon, for instance, reportedly said, "Let small celery wreaths gird our brow as we celebrate a feast to honor Dionysos" (Athenaios 15.674c). Pliny reported that a wreath of fresh celery had the honor of crowning the victors in the sacred games of Nemea in the Peloponnese.

Whereas Pliny called celery *apium*, it was known in ancient Greek as *selinon*, the root for English "celery." Homer had referred to it as *selinon* and described it as growing on the mythic isle of the nymph Calypso, who had once bewitched Odysseus and held him captive for years. Celery consequently was reputed as a force for romantically luring a desired one.

Although Pliny complained that celery seed required at least forty days to sprout and thus was the slowest, most difficult garden plant to cultivate, it did not fail to appear in every ancient herb garden. As archaeobotanical finds now show, the Romans even planted it in the gardens of castles and fortressed villages in their conquered provinces.

Pliny advised that sickened fish could be revived with celery, advice that could have been of considerable consequence at the time for the proprietors of the great—and numerous—fish tanks and ponds surrounding the villas south of ancient Rome.

CELERY *Apium graveolens* (Apiaceae)
Hayne, vol. 7, pl. 24

Apium graveolens

chamomile

To relieve headache, the ancients would place a crown of chamomile on the head. It was braided with fresh or dried blossoms, depending on the season. This was a decorative way to use the aromatic, soothing fragrance of the tender white flowers that still have appeal today.

Matricaria recutita (wild chamomile or so-called "German chamomile") is easy to confuse with "Roman chamomile" (*Chamaemelum nobile*). The name *chamomilla*, which turns up for the first time in an eleventh-century edition of Dioscorides' pharmacology manual, is adapted from the Greek word *chamaimelon*. Translated literally, it means "low-growing apple," which must have meant that the scent was reminiscent of apples to those giving names. Both "German" and "Roman" chamomile have fragrance and flavor, although, generally, the Roman has a stronger fragrance than its counterpart. Adding to the confusion, both the Greek physician Dioscorides and the Roman natural historian Pliny list still more names for chamomile. Waxing poetic, they called it "small spring blossom," "little white flower," or "apple bloomlet," without making clear just which variety of chamomile they meant each time.

Both German chamomile and the Roman variety prove useful in the apothecary. Pliny cited the example of Asclepiades of Bythinia, a reputed surgeon and gynecologist of the first century B.C., who strongly recommended the active agents in chamomile to his patients and colleagues. Contrary to the present practice of using only the blossom, the ancients used chamomile's leaves and the rhizome as well. Both parts were thought to produce a warming effect. In springtime physicians gathered the leaves, which they crushed to make wafers to treat snakebite. A mixture of crushed blossoms and leaves with the ground rhizomes of chamomile produced a highly recommended tea or a therapeutic bath, believed to work just as well in relieving menstrual difficulties as for gall bladder and liver ailments, kidney stones, or inflammations of the bladder. A salve made from olive oil and the blossoms of chamomile was a popular remedy in antiquity for periodic fevers. Blossoms and leaves harvested in summer were preserved by drying, then pulverized and shaped into wafers.

These applications coincide closely with the theories of natural healing today, which employ chamomile externally for inflammations and internally for cramps and gastrointestinal disorders. Superficial skin injuries also respond well to the antiseptic and soothing agents in chamomile blossoms. In antiquity, as today, chamomile was an effective healing agent for inflammations of the eye. Recent studies confirm that the compresses prescribed by ancient physicians proved effective at reducing pain because they effectively counteract inflammations.

CHAMOMILE *Chamaemelum nobile = Anthemis nobilis*
(Asteraceae)
Nees van Esenbeck, no. 245

Anthemis nobilis L.

chicory

Horace, the renowned Roman poet, prays in his *Ode to Apollo* (1.31) for the gods to grant him in old age yet a bit of lust for life and an ability to enjoy the bitter taste of chicory. With its lovely blue flowers, the plant was grown in virtually every house and herb garden in antiquity. Native to Europe, Asia Minor (present-day Turkey), and North Africa, chicory manages to survive in any stony field or dumping ground and grows modestly by the roadside. In time it was introduced in the Far East as well as to North and South America. The Romans called it *intubus* and, according to Pliny, adopted the term *cichorium* from Egypt, where it enjoyed equal popularity as both a vegetable and a medicinal plant. He also cited Egyptian sages, whom he called magicians, who extolled one particular, now long-forgotten use for chicory: people, it was said, could make themselves more popular in social settings by rubbing the entire body with a mixture of olive oil and the juice extracted from the whole chicory plant. Thus anointed, they should find it easy to fulfill all their wishes. Chicory had been viewed for centuries as an aphrodisiac, and lovers would give its seeds to each other to heighten their mutual attraction (Pliny *Natural History* 20.30).

Pliny's list of the medicinal uses for chicory grew so long that he ended up declaring it a panacea. He recommended chicory for all stomach problems and considered chicory root cooked in a barley soup as treatment for the stomach. He assured readers that it worked for the liver and kidneys as well. So long as jaundice was not accompanied by fever, he counseled drinking boiled chicory juice, preferably mixed with honey (*Natural History* 20.30).

One of Pliny's descriptions seems to refer to the now common cultivation of the popular white buds of chicory, which are forced from its roots in darkness. To ensure that spring chicory achieved a shiny white color, he suggested sprinkling beach sand into the heart of the plant as soon as it began to grow (*Natural History* 19.129).

Pliny's contemporary Dioscorides recommended the wide-leafed, sweet-smelling garden chicory for a weak, upset stomach because of its cooling, astringent action. He even claimed that a puree made from its leaves and roots could heal scorpion bites.

In his cookbook Apicius gave a chicory recipe in which chicory is prepared with a sauce composed of oil; vinegar; the salty, fishy condiment *garum*; fruit juice; honey; a bit of fresh cheese; and a teaspoon each of spearmint and lovage. He called it a noteworthy dish!

CHICORY *Cichorium intybus* (Asteraceae)
Nees van Esenbeck, no. 248

Cichorium Intybus.

clover

The astonishingly pleasant fragrance of this yellow- or white-blossoming clover variety caught the attention of Egyptians, Greeks, and Romans very early and won the plant its name. Called honey clover, it is a composite of the Greek terms *meli* (honey) and *lotos* (clover). From western China, *Melilotus* migrated across Asia to Western Europe and, accompanying human cultures, became naturalized in North America.

Dioscorides, the physician from Asia Minor, and his contemporary in the first century A.D., the Roman natural historian Pliny, agreed that the best yellow sweet clover grew in Attica, Greece, and in the vicinity of Nola, near Naples in southern Italy. "The saffron-colored variety is preferred," said Pliny, "although in Italy the white is the most pleasant-smelling" (*Natural History* 21.37).

The fine aroma of the plant grows still stronger on drying. Thus the blossoming branches were an ideal material for weaving the wreaths to be worn at household celebrations and banquets. Pliny referred to yellow sweet clover wreaths as "*sertula campana*," or garlands of blossoms from Campania, the region south of Naples.

Greek sages describe a mighty plane tree (presumably the genus *Platanus*) in the vicinity of Sparta, hallowed for the memory of the marriage of Menelaos to beautiful Helen. In the shade of its leafy branches the young maidens of the region would meet, anoint the tree trunk with precious oils, and in summertime deck its branches with wreaths of yellow sweet clover.

The plant had numerous medicinal applications. Dioscorides recommended cooking the leaves and blossoms of yellow sweet clover in wine and applying it as a compress to alleviate sores and abscesses. Swollen eyes were said to respond to this treatment as well. Others suggested placing the leaves, moistened with rose oil and vinegar—like a compress—on the brow to relieve headaches.

Bladder ailments responded to a tea brewed from yellow sweet clover leaves and the blossoms of one of the mallows. A tincture, produced from this sweet clover and sweet wine, was dripped into the ear passages to alleviate earache.

For thousands of years, yellow sweet clover has provided one of the most frequently used treatments for hemorrhoids and varicose veins, for the herb contains active ingredients with an anti-inflammatory effect. Experience seemed to show that a liquid made from the plant eased heaviness and pain in the legs and relieved congestion as well.

Used not only medicinally, the seeds of yellow sweet clover were often used in antiquity to lend an appealing aroma and taste to soups and drinks.

YELLOW SWEET CLOVER *Melilotus officinalis* (Fabaceae)
Nees van Esenbeck, no. 326

Trifolium Melilotus officinalis.

coriander

Although grown the world over, coriander is not without its detractors. They like to compare the strong scent of the leaves (cilantro) and seeds with the off-putting odor of bedbugs. This is purportedly the reason for its first name in antiquity—*kopis* is the old Greek term for "bug."

Coriander originated in the eastern Mediterranean area and was one of the earliest plants used by humans as a flavoring agent. As recent archaeobotanical finds show, it was among the first wave of cultivated plants, including wheat, flax, and lentils, which came from Palestine to Egypt in prehistoric times and soon found applications in medicine and cookery. Moses, the great prophet and leader of the people of Israel, must have learned about coriander in Egypt. As told in the Bible, he compared heaven-sent manna with coriander seeds.

Pliny knew only cultivated coriander, which he found to be so widely grown in herb gardens that he dispensed with a detailed description of the plant. He did warn, however, against its excessive or continuous use, which might pose a threat to sanity.

Columella recommended sowing in spring as well as fall. If sown in the spring, the seeds would be available by summertime when, lightly pressed and mixed with vinegar, they were used for preserving meat. Ancient cookery would be unimaginable without the famous condiment *garum*, produced from fish and highly aromatic herbs such as coriander.

A favorite Roman recipe was for oven-roasted leg of lamb rubbed with oil and pepper, sprinkled with a mixture of salt and coriander ground in a mortar. Fish could be prepared in similar fashion, carefully cleaned, coated with a mortar-ground mixture of salt and coriander, and then simmered in liquid in a fireproof container.

While coriander was used to conceal the musty taste of old flour, it was also an agreeable addition when baking bread or seasoning a light ale.

Medicinal applications in antiquity included treatment for every kind of stomach or intestinal disorder. Followers of the Greek physician Hippocrates (ca. 460–ca. 377 B.C.) found coriander helpful in relieving heartburn. They prescribed eating both raw and cooked coriander to counteract fainting spells or jaundice, and they recommended the application of its fresh leaves externally as a compress for skin inflammations and purulent sores.

A few leaves taken as dessert, these practitioners believed, could ensure a pleasant night's sleep.

CORIANDER *Coriandrum sativum* (Apiaceae)
Nees van Esenbeck, no. 287

Coriandrum sativum.

cretan dittany

Roman literature and painting paid particular honor to an herb that grew on the famous Greek island of Crete, located between Africa and Europe. Its healing power was so legendary that even the gods headed there for cures from their deadly wounds. Venus would have been helpless to save Aeneas without this miraculous plant from the slopes of Mount Ida. In the *Aeneid* Virgil described the hero's rescue after suffering a battle wound:

> But now, shaken by her son's undeserved suffering, Aeneas's mother Venus picked from Cretan Ida the plant dictamnus, whose stalk is tressed with luxuriant leaves, and whose flower is bright red; it is a fodder well known indeed to the wild goats when the flying arrows stay clinging in their backs. With her form shrouded in a mantle of mist, Venus carried this plant down. . . . And suddenly all the pain which Aeneas had felt vanished, and from deep down in the wound the flow of blood quite ceased; then the arrow-head came away readily in Iapyx's hand, dropping out of its own accord, and forced by no one. Aeneas's strength, fresh as of old, returned to him.
>
> (Virgil *Aeneid* 12.412–24)

The knowledge of the miraculous power of Cretan dittany derives from none other than Aristotle, who was the first to tell how the wild goats of Crete would eat a few leaves of it and immediately be healed when the arrows fell spontaneously from their wounds. Later Dioscorides and Pliny both mentioned these herbally well-informed goats, and in the seventeenth and eighteenth centuries travel accounts from Crete still showed goats munching on this particular oregano.

The appearance of this plant in the vicinity of Zeus's (Roman, Jupiter) birthplace, the Dittany Mountains of Crete, earned the plant the name *dictamnus* in antiquity, and it has come down to us as *Origanum dictamnus*. The religious significance of its mythic mountain location no doubt helped its reputation for magical powers.

From the aromatically scented plant people sought relief not just from arrow wounds but also from poisonous animal bites. In antiquity, women counted on it for help in childbirth and for gynecological complaints, believing that the goddesses Artemis and Hecate, who presided over these matters, considered dittany sacred.

From early on the dwarf plant was a coveted commodity for export, but one with a caveat: Although *Origanum dictamnus* was planted in gardens far from Crete, it was believed that its magical powers declined markedly beyond Crete's shores, a notion Pliny dismissed as prejudice.

CRETAN DITTANY *Origanum dictamnus* (Lamiaceae)
Curtis, vol. 9, no. 298

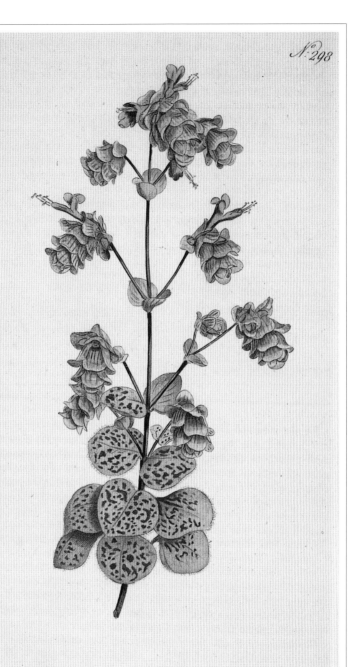

Pub. by W. Curtis S.ᵗ Geo Crescent Apr. 1.1795

cumin

Excavations in Egypt have shown that cumin, originally indigenous to Turkistan, was brought very early to the Nile region and Ethiopia. The flavorful seeds soon turned up in Persia, where the imported spice was preferred at court to the local product. Centuries later the Romans, upon being introduced to cumin in Greece, also praised Egyptian and Ethiopian cumin.

As is well known from the Greek comedies, cumin was one of the most common kitchen staples, along with greens, salt, water, and oil. Cumin and salt were proverbial terms for good friendship. Yet the tiny seeds were also at the root of a Roman proverb that considered a miser a "cumin splitter." Regardless, as reported by Dioscorides and Pliny, if your cumin harvest were unsatisfactory, you could dependably find the imported herb—with its special qualities when produced in Egypt, Asia Minor, southern Italy, or Spain—at Greek and Roman markets.

Not just a popular cooking herb, cumin also had medicinal applications. However, according to Theophrastos, the farmer must mutter oaths and curses while planting the seed to safeguard its magical powers and drive out evil spirits. Cumin ranked among the best medicines for the stomach. Pliny claimed there was no finer potherb for treating nausea. Its seeds contain essential oils with excellent antispasmodic properties, which stimulate the secretion of gall and the action of the kidneys, relieve flatulence, and aid digestion. Roman doctors used to toast cumin seeds and administer them, mixed in wine, for fainting spells, liver ailments, and to treat tinnitus. A small sack containing cumin seed was placed on the belly of a child suffering from stomachache.

Cumin had additional uses. It was believed that a woman would conceive more readily if the smell of cumin with its magical power wafted about her nose during intercourse. When the plant was smoked, the oil released was effective for disinfecting rooms. Poets and thinkers agreed that cumin had the power to whiten reddened cheeks. The story was told in Rome, for instance, that the pupils of the noted rhetorician Porcius Latro chewed cumin seeds to acquire the pallor associated with the lengthy study he seemed to require.

Apicius's famous cookbook was about taste, not pallor. Its recipes for nearly all popular sweet-and-sour sauces were flavored with cumin, whether plum sauce for roast duck, date sauce for guinea hen, or squash-date-peach sauce for roast chicken. There is a recipe worthy of imitation for an omelet with peaches served with a cumin sauce. Unimaginable without the delicate flavor of cumin were dishes with oysters and fish, or vegetables like beans, peas, artichokes, lentils, and squash (*Lagenaria siceraria*).

CUMIN *Cuminum cyminum* (Apiaceae)
Nees van Esenbeck, no. 288

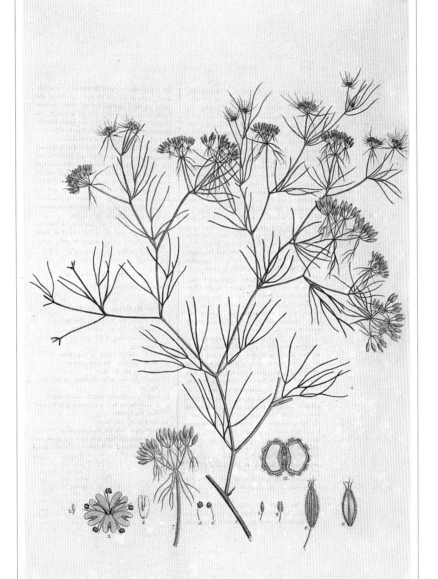

Cuminum Cyminum Lin.

dill and fennel

Dill and fennel are relatives with a strong family resemblance. Both served to flavor Romans' soups, especially one described in the cookbook of Apicius for the wonderful source of all minestrones, that mixture of peas, beans, fresh vegetables, sprigs of dill, and the seeds of fennel. The two herbs lent their superb flavors to the ancient, ubiquitous condiment *garum*. Roman cooks were fond of plucking sprigs of fresh dill from herb gardens to add refinement to recipes for boar, chicken, or peas.

Fennel appeared on Roman tables as a fresh green, but, for the most part, the spicy seeds became more popular and were used to flavor pungent sauces or top the crusts of fresh-baked breads. Both the green stalks of fennel and the seeds were indispensable in autumn for pickling olives.

The ancient world believed that snakes had discovered the healing powers of fennel: After the reptiles sloughed their skin, they supposedly rubbed against fennel plants to strengthen their eyesight. In fact, even today medicinal healers treat tired eyes or visual weakness with an eyewash of fennel water.

With its attractive umbrella of yellow blossoms and delicately fragrant green leaves, dill was a popular decorative plant from which splendid wreaths could be made to honor the god Bacchus (Dionysos). Both fennel and dill originated in the Middle East and spread from there very early; much later they became naturalized in North America. Regardless of location or time, both have been highly prized medicinal herbs whose seeds can relax the gastrointestinal system and relieve stomachache and flatulence; both were also trusted to promote lactation in nursing mothers. Dried dill was in great demand in ancient Italy as an essential ingredient in the popular and affordable herbal cheese called *moretum*. Happy the man who could market dill from his garden, as Columella tells us in his song on farming:

> Garlic with onions join, and with the dill
> Ceres' blue poppy, and to market bring
> Still fresh the close-packed bunches and, with wares
> All sold, to Fortune solemn praises sing,
> And to your garden home rejoicing go.
> (Columella *On Agriculture* 10.315–19)

Dill and Fennel
Anethum graveolens and *Foeniculum vulgare* (Apiaceae)
Foeniculum vulgare: Nees van Esenbeck, no. 277

Anetum foeniculum

elecampane

It became fashionable in ancient Rome to eat the rootstock of elecampane as a delicacy sweetened with honey after Julia, daughter of Caesar Augustus, began the trend of enjoying this sweet on a daily basis. It is small wonder that other Romans also cultivated elecampane in small plots for pleasure and profit.

Indigenous to Central Asia, elecampane came to be cultivated throughout the Mediterranean over the centuries and spread worldwide. Its roots are not only a source for sweet snacks but also of diverse medicines. To produce them, the pleasantly aromatic root is dried and ground to a powder. Once boiled in water and sweetened with honey, the mixture helped alleviate coughing, shortness of breath, cramps, flatulence, and the dreaded bites of wild animals. Pliny reported that elecampane fortified the teeth— but only if the excavated plant root had had no further contact with the soil. He listed various methods for sweetening the bitter root to make it tolerable: Knead the pulverized dried root with honey and mix it with raisins and dates; to vary the taste, prepare the powder with plums, thyme, and pepper—these would strengthen the weak stomach (*Natural History* 19.29).

Even more precise directions for preserving elecampane came from the practitioner Columella. He did not dig up the roots until they were fully ripe in October. Then, after cleaning the sand and soil off with a rough linen cloth or a goat-hair towel, he peeled the roots, cut them into finger-length slices, and cooked them in vinegar and water until they were soft and had lost their bitterness. Next the slices were dried in the shade for three days. Finally, they were moistened either with sweet wine or brine, depending on the planned use (*On agriculture* 12.48).

The Greek natural historian Theophrastos said that the name *inula* is derived from the Greek word meaning "to heal" and refers to the medicinal effect of the roots. Ancient myths tell how this plant, with its lovely yellow blossoms, arose from the tears shed by Helen of Troy when Menelaos's steersman died. The Romans often added *campana* to the name *inula*, referring to the rich landscape of Campania near Naples, which was particularly suitable for the plant's cultivation. This ancient Roman designation, *Inula campana*, is reflected in the English term "elecampane." Carolus Linnaeus, however, in systematizing botanical names in the eighteenth century, went back to the Greek sources for the taxonomic name *Inula helenium*.

ELECAMPANE *Inula helenium* (Asteraceae)
Nees van Esenbeck, no. 240

Inula Helenium.

fenugreek

Theophrastos thought a fenugreek seed pod looked like "goat's horn" and named the plant that; Dioscorides called it "ox horn" for the same reason. Fenugreek's seed pods, which can reach nearly five inches (13 cm) in length, each conceal ten to twenty seeds. The square yellow-brown seeds are significantly rich in vitamins, protein, calcium, fats, essential oils, iron, and bitter essences and are highly valuable for culinary and medicinal uses.

A member of the pea family, fenugreek is native to the eastern Mediterranean and to Central Asia. Its cultivation in Asia Minor (present-day Turkey), Egypt, and western India extends far back in time.

The seeds have been found in Egyptian graves as early as the third millennium B.C., possibly to provide nourishment for the dead in the afterlife. Seed remains were also found in the grave of Pharaoh Tutankhamen. Early papyrus book scrolls contain instructions for extracting a cosmetic oil from the seeds; the wondrous product was described in these terms in the ancient text: "When one rubs down the body therewith, the result is a beautification of the skin and a cleansing of all skin impurities as well as any sign of age that may have been on the body. It has been tried innumerable times, with remarkable success."

It was apparently in Greece that the Romans became acquainted with this plant, which they named *foenum graecum*, "Greek hay." This is the root for the English term "fenugreek."

Because their heavy oil content makes the seeds particularly nutritious, they became a popular addition in Roman times to the diet for convalescents. They were given to women, for instance, to hasten recovery from childbirth. Fenugreek was known to promote lactation during breastfeeding as well.

Columella urged gardeners to plant "Greek hay" in autumn when day and night were of equal length and to use the dried, roasted seeds to make a vegetable oil. Dioscorides had high praise for an oil made with fenugreek, which he recommended as most effective for treating any hardening of the womb or for so-called dry births. His recipe called for softening nine pounds (ca. 4 kg) of fenugreek with five pounds of oil and two pounds (1 kg) of sedge for seven days. The combination was to be stirred daily, then strained and preserved. He cautioned his readers to select fresh oil that does not smell too strongly of fenugreek but makes the hands slippery and has a bittersweet taste, for this type is the best.

Current medical theory holds that fenugreek seed can alleviate pain, promote metabolism, and stimulate appetites. Fenugreek was a primary ingredient in the famous nineteenth-century tonic of Lydia Pinkham.

Fenugreek *Trigonella foenum-graecum* (Fabaceae)
Nees van Esenbeck, no. 325

Trigonella foenum graecum Lin.

garlic and onion

Garlic and onion were indispensable as both food and medicine in antiquity. Even the smallest herb garden reserved some space for each. Both have been cultivated for so long that all wild forms have long since disappeared, but the place of origin is believed to be Central Asia. Although difficult to see at first glance, both belong to the noble family of the lily. More obvious is the characteristic smell and taste, normally stronger in garlic than onion.

The odors and tastes of different alliums are caused by differing compounds of sulfur and carbon, which are typical of this genus of plant. These substances, however, also account for their medicinal value because they counteract harmful bacteria in the stomach and intestines.

Because it is healthful and tasty, garlic has many fans; but its unpleasant smell has earned it just as many enemies. This has always been the case, even in ancient Rome. "It causes a repellant breath," Pliny complained in *Natural History* (19.34), but he added, "It is said to be useful in many different country remedies." So dreaded was this "foul odor" in Rome that access to certain temples was restricted to those who had not eaten garlic. Before cleaning hives, beekeepers were advised to refrain from all foods that, like onion and garlic, are associated with "stinking exhalations."

As an aphrodisiac, on the other hand, the alliums had more appeal. In particular, onions from the Greek area of Megara reportedly aroused men and prepared them for love-making. Pliny favored garlic, which he recommended in a love potion mixed with coriander and dissolved in wine. He was somewhat amazed that the Egyptians swore oaths on the onion and garlic as if the plants were equal to gods; in fact, the Egyptians did ascribe magical force to both.

The Romans relied more on the medicinal power of the plant. To treat the most diverse ailments, Pliny counted dozens of recipes for garlic alone, including a bean soup with garlic to treat dizzy spells; a puree from garlic and oregano to counteract facial freckles; and garlic, burned to ash and mixed with honey, to cure blue spots.

Garlic and onion served as a cure-all in rural areas, where they were also food staples for those common folk. By contrast, the use of garlic and onion in the fine urban cooking of imperial Rome was frowned upon. Among the recipes in the cookbook of that period by Apicius there are a few recipes that use onions, but only a single sauce calls for a touch of garlic!

GARLIC and ONION
Allium sativum and *Allium cepa* (Alliaceae)
Allium sativum: Nees van Esenbeck, no. 5

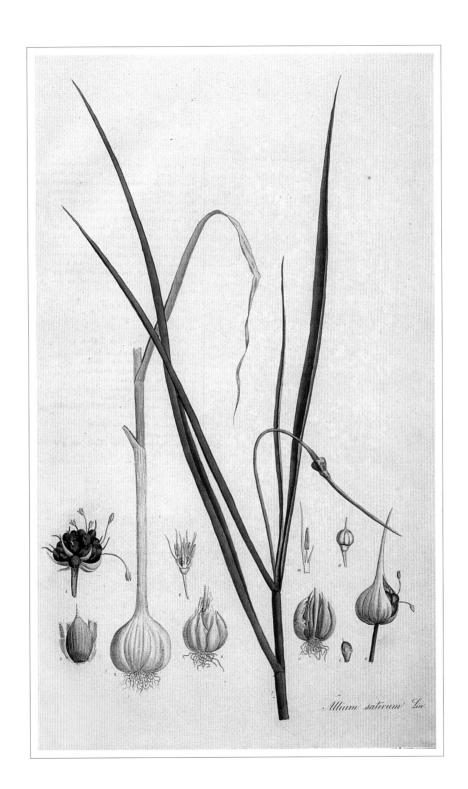

Allium sativum Lin.

hollyhock

First and largest of the malvaceous plants native to the Mediterranean and cultivated since antiquity was the hollyhock. Its blossoms, along with those of the lily and rose, were among the most decorative in the Roman garden. Tinted pinkish to dark violet, its flowers can be identified in a few ancient garden murals. Admired for its beauty, hollyhock was an important edible plant that mythology endowed with religious significance as well. The tasty buds, blossoms, and fruit of the various malvaceous plants were hailed as a basic food found everywhere, given by the gods as a means of assuaging hunger and thirst. Consequently, at an annual thanksgiving harvest celebration, the ancient Greeks sacrificed blooming, fruit-bearing mallows on the altar of Apollo at Delos.

The beautiful hollyhock was also a beneficial medicinal plant. Its healing properties were eclipsed, however, by those of its relative, marsh mallow (*Althaea officinalis*). *Althaea*, believed to come from the ancient Greek word meaning "to heal," is capable of treating many illnesses. The leaves and blossoms were of value, but the roots proved the most useful in cases of indigestion, diarrhea, inflammations, toothache, and earache. The viscous substances from this entire group of plants remain a proven remedy for coughs and all kinds of bronchial inflammations.

Pliny dwelt at surprising length on malvaceous plants in *Natural History*, citing four different wild and cultivated varieties; because—in his view—their effects did not vary, he provided no closer description. A small glass of the juice of mallow daily, he advised, would protect against all illness, no matter which of the mallows one used (*Natural History* 20.84).

Juices, tinctures, and compresses from the leaves of malvaceous plants offered relief from severe burns, scaly skin, sores, and painful blisters. It was possible to use them preventively; according to Pliny "People who rub themselves with grated mallow, of any variety, or carry a twig of the plant on their person, are not stung by insects." He also recommended the roots to fortify the teeth and relieve toothache. If eaten raw, the seeds acted as a strong aphrodisiac; if cooked, they offered relief to depressives, the mentally unstable, and epileptics (*Natural History* 20.84).

The blossoms and fruit of mallows were popular in Roman cooking as a vegetable. In the cookbook of Apicius various recipes call for combinations of their blossoms with other vegetables and greens, such as in a stuffing for roast suckling pig. A dish made up of mallow blossoms, peas, and greens served with olive oil was named for Emperor Vitellius (A.D. 15–69), whose appetite, according to contemporary chronicles, knew no bounds.

MALLOW *Alcea rosea* (Malvaceae)
Nees van Esenbeck, no. 416

Alcea rosea.

horehound

Common horehound has a long pedigree as a healing plant. Its older name, "seed of Horus," suggests that it was already known in pharaonic Egypt. Indeed, horehound leaves, gathered in blooming season, have been recognized as a healing agent since antiquity.

Originating in the southern Mediterranean, common horehound was cultivated very early and often ran wild; by the Middle Ages it had become a plant linked to human settlements. Requiring nitrogen and warmth, it spread quickly east to Central Asia and west to Europe and later naturalized in North and South America. Along with the mints and bee balm, it belongs to the Lamiaceae family, and its tiny blossoms are pollinated exclusively by smaller varieties of bees.

Its genus name *Marrubium* comes undoubtedly from the Hebrew language and is composed of the words *mar* for "bitter" and *rob*, "very" or "very much," and thus means "very bitter." The plant has, however, a pleasantly balsamic aroma. Its high content of tannic acid and bitter essences staves off all kinds of pests and parasites. This may have been why the Roman farmer Columella recommended periodic watering of planted beds with a decoction of common horehound to keep other plants free of lice and mites.

Although the plant has become less common today, Pliny said that "the plant is too well known to require a description. It is recommended by most physicians as one of the best herbs. Leaves and seeds, grated together, work against snakebite, pains in chest and side, and old coughs." For heavy coughs, he prescribed a mixture of the fresh seeds of common horehound with salt and oil, brought to a boil, and consumed on an empty stomach. For cramps and nervous disorders he advised drinking a juice pressed from the leaves and mixed with vinegar and honey (*Natural History* 20.89).

Dioscorides, his contemporary from Asia Minor (present-day Turkey), described common horehound as a branching shrub with rough, rounded, wrinkled leaves with a bitter taste. From its seeds, raw or cooked, he recommended pressing the juice, mixing it with honey, and consuming the mixture to ease coughing, whooping cough, and asthma—a use that is common in alternative healing today.

Before describing its preparation, Columella wrote that "many consider horehound wine effective for treating all internal ailments" (*On agriculture* 12.32). In fact, because the tannic acid and bitter essences found in the plant's foliage stimulate the flow of bile and stomach secretions, its leaves are still used medicinally for loss of appetite, heartburn, and indigestion. However, its best-known use is as a remedy for throat irritation and as an expectorant.

COMMON HOREHOUND *Marrubium vulgare* (Lamiaceae)
Nees van Esenbeck, no. 174

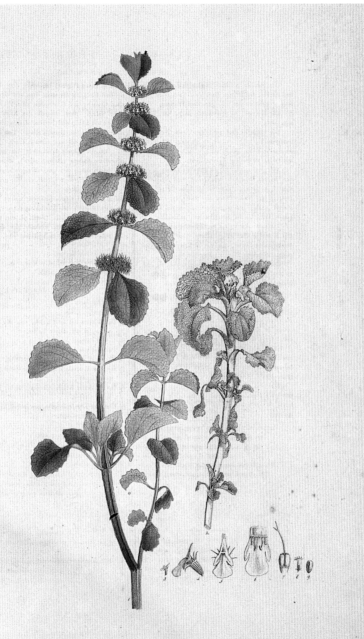

Marrubium vulgare Lin.

hyssop

Hyssop was a most versatile plant with a long, interesting history. Very early Asian cults may have used it to prevent the clotting of sacrificial blood. The Bible describes the use of its branches for the ritual cleansing of lepers. When preparing for the exodus from Egypt, Moses ordered the Israelites to mark their homes' thresholds and doorposts with hyssop twigs, after dipping them in the blood of lambs slaughtered for the ritual meal. The Biblical name *esob* became the Greek *hyssopos*, which is still the plant's name, with only slight alterations in many languages.

The physician Dioscorides thought hyssop a very valuable medicinal plant with multiple uses, although he differentiated between the wild and cultivated varieties. He recommended a heated concoction of hyssop, figs, water, and honey as an excellent treatment for lung inflammations, asthma, chronic cough, shortness of breath, and colds. As a cleansing agent for stomach or intestinal disorders, he prescribed a stock made from hyssop, green figs, a garden cress (most likely *Nasturtium officinale*), and orrisroot. Hyssop boiled with vinegar was an effective mouthwash and was said to soothe toothache. Similar prescriptions are listed by Pliny (*Natural History* 20.51), who thought bad breath a most offensive evil and urged the use of hyssop as its cure. He called for hyssop in cases of gastrointestinal distress, rheumatism, and coughing. Columella praised a root wine made from the juice of grapes and twigs of hyssop called *glechonites*, which was popularly taken as a digestive after overeating.

A similar purpose was served by the spiced, cooked salts served after festive Roman banquets to stimulate the gastrointestinal process. These same salts were also eaten to prevent all manner of illness and to ward off the dreaded plague. A recipe preserved in Apicius's cookbook for preparing such a salt includes many costly ingredients, such as saffron, pepper, ginger, and hyssop. For this purpose, the hyssop was special-ordered from the distant Greek island of Crete and not merely plucked from cook's own garden. Combined with salt—another valuable ingredient—the above spices were placed in a clay pot, covered with straw, and heated in the flames until the salt stopped crackling.

The leaves of hyssop have the greatest concentration of the oils that lend the plant its camphorlike aroma. Because of its aromatic smell, the plant was used to conceal disagreeable odors. The handy plant is easily grown from seed and reaches a fairly ripe age.

It seems likely that the ancient landscape artists, with their love of varying shades of green, also chose the distinctive blue-gray hyssop to frame their plant beds, a practice later continued in Europe's medieval cloister gardens.

Hyssop *Hyssopus officinalis* (Lamiaceae)
Nees van Esenbeck, no. 171

Hyssopus officinalis.

iris

"Heavenly, wondrous, cleansing iris," the pharmacologist Dioscorides called this plant with its comely blossoms. The Romans assumed its Greek name, which recalled Iris, the messenger of the gods, who flew over the rainbow to deliver messages, thereby linking heaven and earth.

Ancient physicians and naturalists were less interested in the fine blossom than in the splendidly aromatic rootstock. Most coveted were the rhizomes of orrisroot, which had to be dug up in a highly mysterious manner before being put to medical or cosmetic use. Theophrastos explained that one had to sprinkle honey water all around the rootstock three months before orrisroot could be unearthed in order to reconcile the earth. Then three rings were made with a sword around the plant, and when the root was finally dug out, it had to be raised toward heaven. Two centuries later Pliny complicated things still further by claming that only a chaste person could extract the rhizome; they must use their left hand while naming aloud the person who was to benefit from its healing power! Finally unearthed, the rhizome was to be dried in the shade, strung on a string, and thus preserved. Its quality was rated according to pleasant aroma and bright color (*Natural History* 21.19).

The rhizomes, also called "violet roots" for their agreeable fragrance, were placed around the neck of a teething baby, partly as talisman and partly so the child could chew on it to ease teething pain; this is sometimes still done today. The ancients would also mix honey with the grated rhizome and administer it as a laxative. They might prepare a drink to soothe a cough, stomachache, or flatulence. Mixed with vinegar, the powder was consumed for pains in the spleen. Orrisroot could be chewed to sweeten the breath and eradicate odor from perspiration. A paste from a bit of wine and powdered rhizome was applied to warts and corns as a cure.

Most important, though, were the cosmetic and medicinal uses of the aromatic oils and salves and the popular perfume obtained from the dried rhizomes of this iris. The oil was said to help with such diverse ailments as inflammations, constipation, tinnitus, chronic colds, shortness of breath, and nausea. A salve extracted from the orrisroot rhizome was a highly regarded pain killer, thought effective during childbirth. Iris perfume was not especially costly and quite popular in ancient Rome. Sweet scents played an important role in everyday life to camouflage the many foul odors suspended in the air.

ORRISROOT *Iris* × *germanica* var. *florentina* (Iridaceae)
Curtis, vol. 16, no. 671

Syd. Edwards del.   Pub. by T. Curtis, St. Geo: Crescent Aug. 1. 1803.   F. Sansom sculp.

juniper

The Mediterranean area, with its relatively mild, moist winters, is never totally drained of all nature's color, but its peoples value evergreen plants just the same. In antiquity, when an evergreen possessed a strong aromatic scent, as is the case with juniper, divine power was easily associated with a plant. This was particularly true for juniper, which has another peculiar trait: Junipers often bear two generations of cones on its branches at all times, a trait believed to be a sign of extraordinary vigor, and one that symbolized continuous renewal and long life. New green "berries," actually small capsules, share the branch alongside their more mature shiny blue- to purplish-black mature cones, which achieve full ripeness during the second year.

Throughout the world there are fifty or more different juniper species, some hovering close to the ground, and some rising to tree height, but for the most part they occur as shrubs, which often form impenetrable thickets. Some junipers are said to live for two thousand years. *Juniperus communis* and its relatives, the cedar juniper (*Juniperus oxycedrus*) and Phoenician juniper (*Juniperus phoenicea*), grow throughout the Mediterranean area, but not in southern Palestine or Egypt. Yet we know that the fleshy cones' varied uses were known to the Egyptians: Junipers "berries" were used to perfume mummies and for ritual practices, and their restorative aroma

had a religious significance. They had a germicidal effect and were used for healing. Since prehistoric time juniper "berries" were, in fact, an important commodity sold to Egypt by countries in the northern and eastern Mediterranean. They provided a lucrative business, packaged easily, and were durable.

Juniper "berries" figured prominently as a drug in all of ancient medicine: Their pharmacological effect was based on their high essential-oil content. The Romans used the "berries" for stomachache and coughs. Properties in the oil produced a diuretic effect and thus the "berries" were taken for kidney ailments; when administered in higher doses, they could provoke uterine bleeding and thereby end an unwanted pregnancy.

In Roman cooking juniper "berries" were among the basic ingredients in all preparations of game. For an especially popular sauce with game dishes, Apicius, the sauce expert in imperial Rome, recommended a mixture of herbs and juniper "berries," dried and ground to a powder, noting that this should always be kept on hand. To prepare the mixture, combine one teaspoon each of pepper, rue, lovage, celery seed, thyme, and spearmint with three teaspoons of juniper "berries." To make the sauce, blend one teaspoon of honey and a cup of *oxygarum* into the herb powder.

COMMON JUNIPER *Juniperus communis* (Cupressaceae)
Nees van Esenbeck, no. 86

Juniperus communis

lovage

Lovage was a much loved kitchen herb and in great demand as a medicinal plant. The plant's home had long been thought to be the Ligurian Apennine range in northern Italy, as claimed by Dioscorides in the first century A.D. In reality it came from Persia (present-day Iran) and was eventually cultivated in the gardens of Europe and is now naturalized in many places in North America. Unfortunately, Italy has yet to turn up archaeobotanical specimens of lovage, and thus debate continues as to whether the *Ligusticum* mentioned so often in the recipes of Apicius truly refers to *Levisticum officinale*.

Dioscorides brewed a juice from the roots of lovage that was said to alleviate pains, flatulence, and snakebite. Its root, with an essential oil, was known for its diuretic effect, and a tea brewed from the root promised relief from urinary illnesses. It was also used to promote digestion.

In addition to its valued roots, the seeds, leaves and stems were widely used in the kitchen. Dioscorides recommended the aromatic leaves of lovage for seasoning or for salad. If we scan Apicius's recipes for references to this aromatic cooking spice, it proves to be among the herbs he used most often. Lovage was greatly admired for its celerylike taste, and Roman cooks used it in all kinds of dishes, such as fish, moray eel, venison, hare, chicken, and dove, as well as with vegetables such as squash, beans, and cabbage. It flavored soups and sauces. The seeds were popularly used as a substitute for more costly pepper.

An especially refined recipe of Apicius's is for a salad of truffles with lovage. The truffles are cut into thin slices and mixed with the finely chopped leaves of lovage and coriander. Then pepper, honey, some fruit juice, oil, and the popular condiment *garum* are stirred into a sauce and poured over the truffles.

Somewhat simpler is the recipe for an appetizer of pickled onions with lovage. One starts by cutting the onions in half and cooking them briefly in wine and olive oil. Add sliced pork liver and chicken wings and continue cooking the whole mixture. Next, combine wine, fruit juice, *garum*, and finely chopped lovage leaves and pour the savory mixture over the onions.

Another unusual recipe from Apicius is for grilled moray eel, with a sauce of dried plums and lovage, seasoned with such customary ingredients as olive oil, *garum*, wine, fruit juice, and pepper.

These are just three examples of the manifold uses of lovage in Roman cuisine.

LOVAGE *Levisticum officinale* (Apiaceae)
Nees van Esenbeck, no. 278

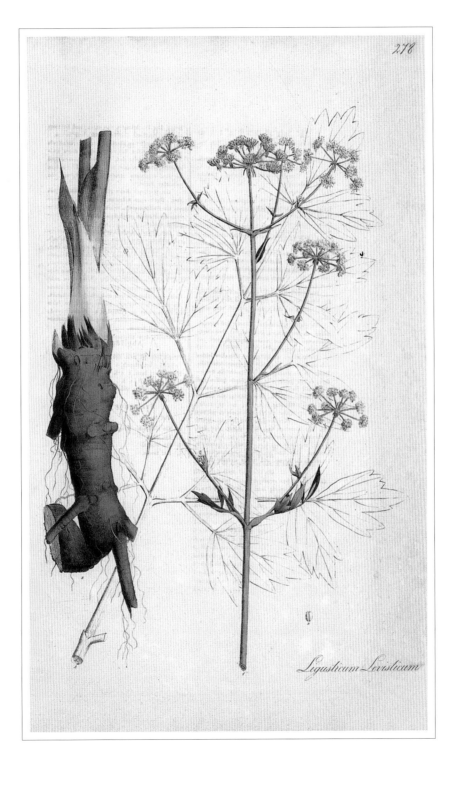

278

Ligusticum Levisticum

marjoram

"Your lips are sweet as marjoram," a youth in ancient Pompeii or Rome might have sighed, and he would be recalling the spicy taste and heady aroma of the plant he might encounter many times daily. Marjoram was used as a culinary herb, an aromatic oil, perfume, bath salt, or beauty salve, as medicine, for garlands on the household altar or wreath on the front door. At day's end, the fragrant herb might crown a guest at a bibulous banquet, although its effectiveness was debated because many herbal experts believed the plant too stimulating for one's nerves.

By contrast, others claimed that marjoram's fragrance promoted especially refreshing sleep. The aroma was thought to protect against many illnesses and other misfortunes. Its versatility won marjoram a following among ancient doctors, who prescribed a marjoram drink to treat dropsy, urinary blockage, and cramps. They considered it useful for tinnitus and toothache. Additionally, the leaf served to ward off ants, according to Pliny.

Marjoram was sacred to the god Hymen, who was responsible for marriages (his mother was Venus, the Greek's Aphrodite, goddess of love). At weddings, the Romans would deck themselves with branches and crowns of marjoram. The Roman poet Catullus (ca. 84–ca. 54 B.C.) provided a lovely image: " . . . Because you bring forth the blossoming maiden, gently on the arms of the man, hail to you, powerful Hymen! Come, bearing the blossom of lovely marjoram about your brow . . . " (Catullus 61.3–7). The marjoram crowns were a sign of love and evoked Hymen, but also Amor, the god of love, who lingered only where marjoram bloomed and perfumed the air. According to ancient poets, Amor glanced away from any man without a crown.

For fragrant marjoram oils and salves—favorite romantic gifts—people of means preferred the products from Cyprus or the Greek isle of Mytilene, where Pliny claimed the finest marjoram was found. In Roman times these gifts became more expensive than comparable products extracted from roses—though still cheaper than saffron, myrrh, or incense. Not only a lover's gift, marjoram was also used for mourning, judging from the many bunches of marjoram found in Roman graves in Egypt.

In antiquity, as today, marjoram was a reputed cooking herb because it could make rich foods easier to digest. It stood among the ten most frequently used herbs in the ancient Roman kitchen. One example from Apicius's cookbook is for a green sauce to garnish cooked meats: Pepper, lovage, marjoram, rue, and onions are finely chopped, mixed with wine, honey, vinegar, and some oil, and stirred to make a cold sauce.

SWEET MARJORAM *Origanum majorana* (Lamiaceae)
Nees van Esenbeck, no. 176

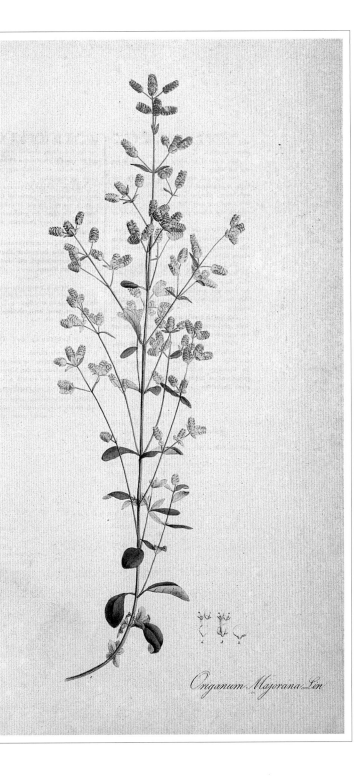

Origanum Majorana Lin.

mugwort

One of its English names, *fly leaf*, conveys a practical use for mugwort that was known even to ancient herbalists: In the evening, hang a bundle of this herb from the ceiling, and before long all insects humming around the room will flock to it. Then carefully pull a sack over the fly-covered twigs and your problem is solved for the day.

The ancients also believed mugwort had magical properties. "On Foot" was the plant's nickname, because all the ancient authors claimed that if you laid a mugwort twig flat in the sandal or tied a few sprigs to a foot or possibly a trouser leg, the herb freed you from fatigue—a person could walk for days at a stretch!

How much the Romans believed in the effectiveness of the herb is clearly seen in another Latin name for it, *valentia* (powerful, capable). They were familiar with the plant's stimulating, antispasmodic, and disinfectant qualities. Its genus name, however, was *Artemisia* because, like its close relative common wormwood, it was considered a gift from Artemis, the goddess favorably inclined toward women. She was supposedly the first to recognize its healing power. An additional English name, motherwort, suggests that mugwort was considered especially effective with feminine health problems during menstruation and childbirth.

Although the shape of the leaves and the inflorescence of mugwort are almost identical with those of common wormwood, the herbs are impossible to confuse because of mugwort's shiny dark-green leaves and their aromatic taste, with none of the bitterness of wormwood. The tips of its shoots, which can be up to ca. 28 inches long (70 cm), are gathered in the blooming season and then dried.

Mugworts are spread over almost all the globe. Its North American Atlantic-coast relatives are distinguished by strong rootstocks. Native Americans from California used *Artemisia ludoviciana* (a sage) for colds, rheumatism, and fever. This native of western North America was used also for ritual smoking. Smoke sacrifices using mugwort were likewise known from ancient Egypt, where they were performed in honor of the goddess Isis.

Mugworts may be one of the world's oldest plants used for medicinal purposes, judging from remains in the prehistoric caves of Lascaux in France. Since antiquity a powder obtained from the roots has been used for epilepsy. Then—and now—people used mugwort to promote digestion, stimulate stomach secretions, cause bile to flow, and to cure the appetite, nausea, diarrhea, and strong halitosis.

Mugworts have always played an important role as a culinary herb as well, serving especially to make fatty meat and oily fish digestible.

MUGWORT *Artemisia vulgaris* (Asteraceae)
Nees van Esenbeck, no. 234

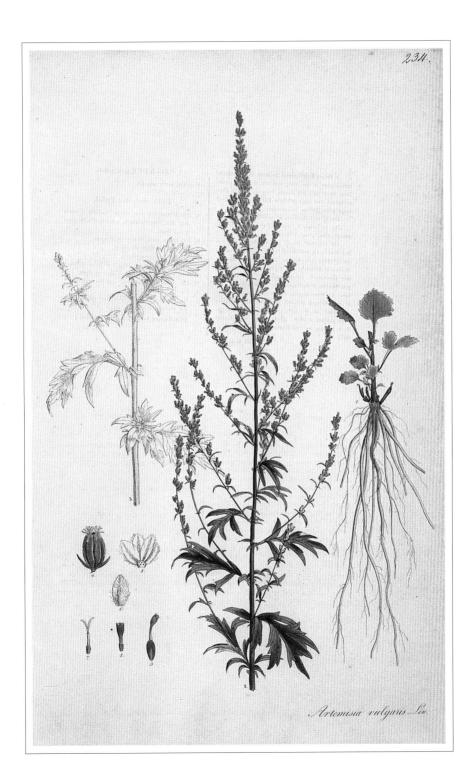

Artemisia vulgaris Lin.

mustard

Ready-to-use mustard in a tube or jar, available at any moment, is taken for granted today. But in antiquity, if you wanted to offer mustard to dinner guests, it was advisable to have the plant—with its pungent seeds—available in your garden. At that time people also used white mustard's young leaves, with a taste reminiscent of garden cress (*Nasturtium officinale*), as a salad or vegetable. Native to the Mediterranean and among the plants longest in cultivation, mustard's true origins are impossible to pinpoint because, in addition to cultivated forms, it grows wild throughout central and northern Europe and has been naturalized in North America.

"Mustard stays just where it's sown, and requires no further care than to be fertilized and cut. It can be sown in autumn or spring. Young mustard plants, which are sown at the onset of winter, however, produce more shoots," wrote the Roman Columella. He went on to deal with the preparation of mustard that was so important for Roman cuisine:

> Clean the mustard seeds thoroughly and pass them through a sieve. Then rinse the mustard seeds in cold water and when they are well washed, let them lie in water for two hours. Remove them and squeeze by hand, put them in a brand-new or thoroughly cleansed mortar, and crush them with a pestle. When the seed is fully pulverized, gather the entire mash in the center of the mortar and press it together with the flat of the hand. Loosen the mass again, insert a few glowing coal chips into it, and wet with soda water to eliminate the bitterness and possible mold from the mustard seeds. Then tip the mortar so that all liquid can flow out. Next strong white vinegar is added and mixed in with the help of the pestle and then strained off. The resulting liquid is an excellent flavoring agent for a turnip dish.

> If you want to serve mustard to dinner guests, then, after the seeds are strained, add the freshest possible pine nuts and almonds and crush them together after vinegar is poured in, . . . Such mustard is not only suitable for sauces but also improves their appearance, for if it is carefully prepared, it has a very attractive shade, for it is brilliantly white.

> (Columella *On agriculture* 12.57)

As cited by Pliny, Pythagoras was the first to demand a thoughtful way of life and the deliberate selection of foods as prerequisites for clear thinking; he believed mustard was the most distinguished of the herbs because no other was so capable of cleansing the nose and the spirit.

WHITE MUSTARD *Sinapis alba* (Brassicaceae)
Nees van Esenbeck, no. 402

Sinapis alba

myrtle

Among the earth's more than one hundred warmth-thriving myrtle varieties, surely none has such regional cultural significance as *Myrtus communis*, a native of the Mediterranean and Asia Minor (present-day Turkey). And, like all evergreen plants with a pleasant aroma, in that region it was a symbol of strong life force.

Persian priests performing divine sacrifices crowned themselves with myrtle branches and stoked the sacred fires with myrtle. In the Old Testament myrtle is celebrated as a sign of peace. In Greek and Roman mythology myrtle was closely associated with the Eastern goddess Astarte (the Greek Aphrodite and the Roman Venus). As protector of all peaceful associations, the myrtle sacred to her became a sign of unification in ancient Athens, and the city's statesmen wore myrtle wreaths as a sign of their worthiness for office. When pronouncing a death sentence, a judge removed the myrtle crown from his head, for myrtle was not meant to be associated with bloody conflict. In Rome myrtle was the sign of a victory won, not by arms, but through persuasion and negotiation. When, after long, unsuccessful, and bloody battles, the Romans and Sabines ended their conflict with a peace treaty—making the founding of the Roman Empire possible —they sealed it under the sacred myrtle tree.

Every April, mothers and young women of Latium—the region around Rome—were said to wash the statues of Venus, deck them with golden bands and fresh roses, and then bathe and adorn themselves with greening myrtle—in remembrance of the goddess that, on emerging naked from the sea, had covered her body with myrtle branches to evade the curious eyes of the satyrs. Myrtle greens were burned in temples as smoke sacrifices, and the Romans adorned household altars and all implements to be used in sacrifices with myrtle branches.

The spicy-sweetish, rounded berries, crowned with the chalice-shaped blossoms, were also widely used in medicine, cosmetics, and cooking. The pea-size berry is either black or white. The black ones, as Columella, Dioscorides, and Pliny agreed, lent themselves better to medicinal use. The method for acquiring the seed was to collect the fruits, remove the seeds from the ripe berries, dry them in the sun, and finally store them in a clay pot in a dry place. Juice squeezed from the fresh myrtle berries was considered especially beneficial to the stomach. Myrtle wine was taken for stomach pains and diarrhea. Myrtle oil squeezed from the leaves was a popular ingredient in cosmetics.

To make a sauce for roast fowl, cooks mixed myrtle berries crushed in a mortar with wine, vinegar, honey, olive oil, and *garum*, and seasoned it with pepper, lovage, celery seed, and spearmint.

MYRTLE *Myrtus communis* (Myrtaceae)
Schlechtendahl, vol. 22, p. 283

T.4. 100.Myrtaceae.

2292. Myrtus communis L. Myrle.

olive

Rich or poor, no one in the ancient Mediterranean could have imagined life without the olive tree. Without olive oil, cooking would be impossible, and even the simplest meal was enriched by pickled olives. Without oil for lamps, nights would remain dark. Resin from the olive tree cured wounds, and people built fires with its wood. Olive oil anointed and cleansed the body. To celebrate victories and signal peace, people placed god-pleasing wreaths made of sprigs from the olive tree on their heads.

Beginning in the late Republic, Roman Italy, thanks to state subsidy, became the most important producer of high-quality olive oil in the Mediterranean. Although olive oil was eventually exported, especially to the northern provinces, olive trees were cultivated in ever greater numbers for private use so that farmers could sustain themselves independently of market conditions, and they were proud to do so.

As usual, Columella was most precise in his instructions to farmers about the planting of trees; he insisted that "all new olive trees, before planting, are to be marked with ochre so that when placed in the ground they are oriented in the same compass direction as they had been in the nursery. Otherwise, if exposed to the effects of different air, contrary to their habit, they would suffer from cold and heat"

(Columella *On trees* 17.4). Perhaps countering the need for such precision, Pliny reported that olive groves were offering such strong tree stock for sale that fruits were ripe for harvest just a year after planting (*Natural History* 15.1).

The olive tree is among the oldest cultivated plants on earth and accordingly had sacred significance. All the ancient authors paid particular attention to it. The physicians among them described its curative properties but differentiated between the fruits of wild and cultivated trees: Oil from the fruits of cultivated trees warmed the body, guarding it against cold, and relieved heat in the head; oil from the fruits of wild trees was used for cleansing the mouth and said to heal rotting gums and secure loosened teeth. A fine paste made from preserved olives would prevent burn blisters and cleanse infected wounds.

Countless recipes handed down from antiquity give instructions for pickling olives. Fennel, celery, rue, and spearmint were popularly used with green olives, while anise and bay laurel leaves were thought to enhance the flavor of black olives.

Olive oil was used for skin care and cleansing and thus took the place of today's soap in the lives of the ancient Greeks and Romans.

OLIVE *Olea europaea* (Oleaceae)
Nees van Esenbeck, no. 212

Olea Europaea

parsley

Even people with no herb garden of their own recognize parsley as a common cooking herb or at least as a decorative garnish for beautifully served food. Indeed, its universal familiarity defies efforts to document exactly how often it turned up in ancient herb beds. A further complication is the ancient nomenclature of the plant: it was dubbed "stone celery," or *petrosellinon*, by the first Greek naturalists, one of which was Theophrastos. The difference is quite obvious between the Roman name for celery (*apium*) and the English word "parsley" (clearly derived from the Greek *petroselinum*). However, parsley's difference from celery is often unclear in the ancient descriptions and troublesome to explain. For help in the matter, we can look forward to seed discoveries and pollen analyses from the fast-developing discipline of archaeobotany.

It is also surprising to find that the ancient world called parsley by the name *stone celery*, for the Italian or flat-leafed variety prospers best in a deeper, nutritious earth and a slightly moist setting with partial shade—not among stones.

Wild-growing parsley is native to southeastern Europe, but for centuries it has also been cultivated throughout the continent as well as in North and South America, Japan, and Australia.

Pliny and Columella had already differentiated the two subspecies that are still in use today—flat-leafed and curly parsley. Throughout the parts of both plants and during each growth phase, parsley stores up essential oil that promotes digestion and acts as a diuretic.

In his pharmacology manual, Dioscorides listed parsley among the different varieties of celery (aptly illustrating the confusion mentioned above), but less as a cooking herb than a healing plant. Like other members of the Apiaceae family—umbrella-shaped plants that include anise, fennel, and actual celery—parsley's fruit yields a useful oil. In antiquity, crumbled fresh leaves were placed on burns and sores to produce a cooling comfort.

In Rome, gladiators purportedly received parsley compresses before combat in the belief that this would redouble their courage and strength.

The roots, which can be dug up in the autumn, were boiled and used for kidney or urinary tract ailments, as well as for gastrointestinal ills.

Columella tells of having lovingly plucked the first ripe olives of the year as early as the end of August and preparing them with herbs, oil, and vinegar, and a small bouquet of fresh parsley as the crowning touch (*On agriculture* 12.49). The gourmet Apicius recommended parsley as an essential flavoring for a delicious, spicy plum sauce to accompany braised venison.

Undoubtedly, parsley was welcome in the herb gardens of antiquity!

PARSLEY *Petroselinum crispum* (Apiaceae)
Nees van Esenbeck, no. 283

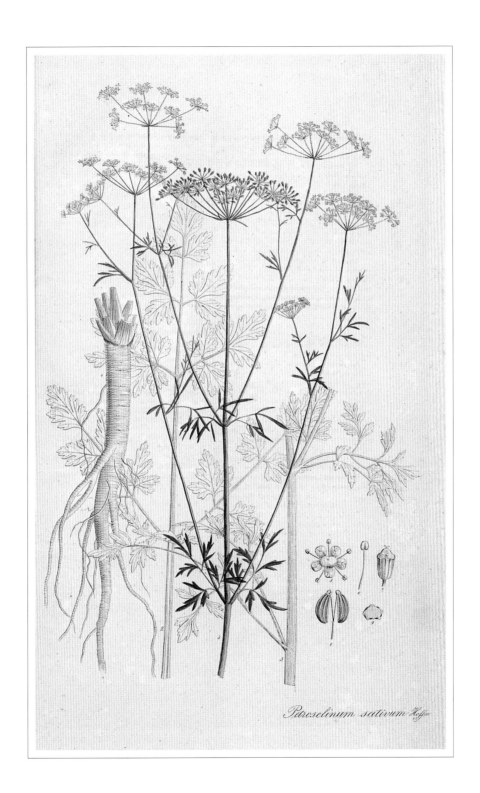

Petroselinum sativum Hoffm.

pennyroyal

From antiquity until the early modern era, pennyroyal was a well-known medicinal plant as well as a popular cooking herb. Then, in the seventeenth century, it retreated into obscurity, pushed aside by peppermint —a cross of other *Mentha* species—which arose by chance in England. Pennyroyal's strong aroma, low height, and tiny leaves always set it apart from the vast number of mint varieties.

Pennyroyal's specific epithet, *pulegium*, probably derives from Latin *pulex* (flea), for its strong odor made the plant useful as a repellant. If available, pennyroyal could still be counted for this handy, pleasant remedy.

Dispersed throughout the Mediterranean and elsewhere in Europe, pennyroyal quickly ran wild in North America after settlers began cultivating it in their gardens.

The smell of pennyroyal would protect a person's head from frost and heat alike, and Pliny instructed that two twigs of pennyroyal placed behind one's ears would prevent harm from the sun. Pliny also quoted Terentius Varro, sage and statesman from the era of Julius Caesar, who urged his readers not to hang any rose crowns in their homes, but rather to hang those made of pennyroyal twigs, which alone had the power to reawaken dormant life spirits and to still or drive away all pain (Pliny *Natural History* 20.54).

Pliny advised casting the grated seeds of pennyroyal on potentially contaminated water to purify it— a sure way to counter any possible health risk. He recommended sniffing finely chopped pennyroyal mixed with some vinegar as a cure for fainting spells. Dried and finely grated, the herb could allegedly fortify the gums; pureed with barley groats, it made a compress to cure all kinds of inflammation; boiled down and used as a bath salt, it relieved itching; and cooked and mixed with vinegar water, it cured nausea, vomiting, and stomachache (*Natural History* 20.54–55). Therefore, it was considered wise always to have the plant available and within easy reach in the garden.

So proverbial was the plant's harmonious qualities in gardens that Cicero once compared the sensitivity of a friend with the nature of pennyroyal.

A recipe preserved in Apicius's cookbook for a squash puree (*Lagenaria siceraria*) flavored with pennyroyal was apparently such a popular dish that it was still being prepared centuries later in the kitchens of medieval cloisters.

PENNYROYAL *Mentha pulegium* (Lamiaceae)
Nees van Esenbeck, no. 165

Mentha Pulegium Lin.

pomegranate

Pomegranates symbolized eternal fruitfulness. They are among the oldest medicinal and cultivated plants of Western Asia. The earliest evidence is a Mesopotamian cult vase of the fourth millennium B.C. from a temple dedicated to the goddess Astarte, a precursor of Greek Aphrodite and Roman Venus. According to legend, the goddess of love planted pomegranate for the first time on the isle of Cyprus.

At the end of the Middle Kingdom, about 1800 B.C., the pomegranate was introduced into Egypt. Its first illustration is found in Karnak in the botanical cabinet of Tutmosis III. Knowledge about the plant and the pharmaceutical effect of its rind was also apparently transmitted at that time: It was already being dispensed, according to papyri regarding medicines that were produced shortly after the plant's introduction. The knowledge and use continue almost unchanged today. The rind of the plant yields an excellent treatment for tapeworm, because alkaloids contained in pomegranate numb the worm's nervous system so that it can no longer cling to the host's intestinal wall, and the worm can be naturally eliminated. Medicinal uses were not restricted to the rind, however; boiling the blossoms produced a mouthwash that was believed to fortify the gums and any loosened teeth.

Pomegranate's gently toothed, light-green leaves were arranged in the floral garlands on the mummy of Pharaoh Tutankhamen, and its shining blossoms continued to decorate the dead in Egypt until Graeco-Roman times. The living apparently appreciated pomegranates greatly, for they frequently appear in wall paintings in Pompeii.

Greek mythology associated pomegranate with Pluto (Hades, god of the Underworld), in whose subterranean garden the plant was believed to grow. Pluto (Hades) captured Proserpina (Persephone), daughter of Ceres (Demeter), the earth mother. In her pain and anger Ceres (Demeter) caused all of earth's plants to dry up until the gods intervened and Pluto (Hades) had to allow Proserpina (Persephone) to return to earth. However, Pluto (Hades) tricked her into eating pomegranate seeds, the food of the dead, thus forcing her to spend one-third of the year in the Underworld with him, when nature was dormant, and two-thirds of the year on earth with her mother, when nature flourished— the mythological explanation for the seasons of the year.

Apicius provided a recipe for a digestive drink popular with the emperor Nero. It was prepared by boiling quince (*Cydonia oblonga*), sorb apple (*Sorbus domestica*), and pomegranate seeds in good fruit juice, pressing the liquid through a fine sieve, and garnishing it with Sicilian sumac (*Rhus coriaria*) and saffron (*Crocus sativus*). Pomegranates were decorative additions to the bowls of fruit that were passed around at the end of a lavish meal, and the sweet seeds were a popular means of quenching the thirst.

POMEGRANATE *Punica granatum* (Punicaceae)
Nees van Esenbeck, no. 301

Punica Granatum.

poppy

A garden in Pompeii or Herculaneum could have two contrasting varieties of poppy planted in its beds. The bright spots of red might come from the fragile blossoms of the corn poppy (*Papaver rhoeas*), which can be seen in the surviving murals along with roses, lilies, and other plants. The wall paintings and mosaics also show the pale violet blossoms and characteristic greenish-blue pods of opium poppy, which has furthermore been documented by pollen traces in excavations. While corn poppy was sown for pure pleasure and decoration, the opium poppy was among the most versatile and mysterious edible plants in the herb bed. The prodigious plant is described in an ancient riddle that is not all that difficult to solve:

> Great is my head, containing many parts;
> Just one foot I have, but that on giant scale;
> I call Sleep my friend, but find no sleep myself.
> (Symphosius *Enigmas* 4.343)

Night, Sleep, and Death, closely associated with the poppy in ancient mythology, adorn themselves with its fruits.

The Roman gardener knew to go early in the morning, when the dew had just dried, to obtain the milky nectar—the beneficent but equally dangerous opium. The ancients believed poppy was a gift of the goddess Ceres (Demeter), who supposedly used the liquid from opium poppies to ease her pain and desperation during her search for her kidnapped daughter, Proserpina (Persephone). The effects of opium had been known since Homer's day. The beautiful Helen, after returning to Sparta from Troy, served her guests a drink made of wine and opium nectar to draw a calming veil over the horrific suffering they had witnessed during the Trojan War.

Realistically, however, opium provided people in antiquity with an easy dose of pain medication within garden's reach. Even though the Romans occasionally went beyond this normal use and, with higher doses, poisoned a fellow human being or—painlessly— themselves, opium did not gain notoriety as a narcotic until many centuries later.

If, on the other hand, Roman gardeners allowed the poppy pods to go to seed in the garden, the black seeds in the clattering fruits would serve to make a wonderfully digestible, nutritious, light and odorless oil that was totally harmless. The black seeds were a welcome addition to fine baked goods, although Pliny cautioned that the cook should first coat the crust with egg yolk to hold the tiny poppy seeds in place. The satirist Petronius (d. A.D. 66), Pliny's contemporary, described an opulent banquet hosted by his character, Trimalchio, who pampered his guests with roast dormouse served in a honey sauce strewn with poppy seeds.

Opium Poppy *Papaver somniferum* (Papaveraceae)
Nees van Esenbeck, no. 405

Papaver Somniferum

rose

It must have been the gentle texture of the petals and their delicate scent that elevated the rose to its enduring prominence in the world of plants.

Wild roses proliferate across the entire northern hemisphere in some two hundred different varieties, of which forty-five are native to Europe.

Even in antiquity there were both the half-full and the full forms of this particular species, which authors like Theophrastos and Pliny called the "sixty-petal rose." They are depicted in astonishingly naturalistic detail in frescoes in the houses at Pompeii. Not only have images survived: actual blossoms, bound together in rose garlands, bouquets, and crowns were preserved in Graeco-Roman tombs, in use since ancient times.

The Greeks first introduced roses to Egypt, where they were cultivated in great numbers by the Roman period. It is said that Kleopatra, the last ruler in the Greek dynasty of the Ptolemies, set out to greet and dazzle Roman military commander Marc Antony in a boat whose decks were strewn with rose petals. Luxury on this scale became the talk of Rome, and imitators were not slow to follow: In winter when no rose bloomed—even in the relatively mild climate of Italy—wealthy Romans ordered entire shiploads of the fragrant blossoms from Egypt to adorn their homes.

The rose's symbolism owes more, however, to the healing properties hidden in its floral petals. Even in antiquity experience had demonstrated the astringent properties of rose petals. Guests at festive celebrations where heavy wine consumption in honor of Bacchus and other gods was the custom were advised to don a crown of roses to guard against headaches. Since fragrances have always enhanced human well-being, these crowns were most pleasant to wear. For the same reason, rose-scented salves became a popular—although expensive—commodity. The scent of the rose has always been sought as perfume.

Novels and stories since antiquity have illustrated the rose's power to resolve life's thorny matters. The flower's importance began with a romantic novel by the poet Apuleius (A.D. ca. 123–ca. 170) telling of a young man named Lucius who, transformed into a donkey, could not break the spell until he had eaten a rose.

All roses, according to legend, were originally white. They turned red only from the blood of Aphrodite, goddess of love, who was pricked by a rose thorn as she rushed to save the dying Adonis. Drops of her blood fell and dyed the rose red; the red rose thereby became the symbol of enduring love, a symbolism still attributed to the rose throughout the world today.

FRENCH ROSE *Rosa gallica* (Rosaceae)
Nees van Esenbeck, no. 303

Rosa gallica Lin

rosemary

As a burnt offering on an altar to the gods, rosemary released a superbly aromatic fragrance to express thanks and appeal for help. Because of the aroma of its resin and root, reminiscent of incense, it became a substitute for that costly substance in smoke-filled temples.

Its fine evergreen twigs proved popular for weaving into the crowns and garlands that were especially obligatory at funeral celebrations. Pliny commented on this important function when he referred to *"Rosmarinum coronarium"* (or rosemary for making crowns).

The poet Horace even claimed that a fragrant crown of evergreen rosemary was preferred by the immortal gods to all other offerings:

> You need make no divine offerings
> Of bloodied beast, if only you crown
> The gods' images with rosemary
> And tender myrtle.
>
> (Horace *Odes* 3.23)

The Greeks used the plant—highly prized for the medicinal properties of its root, leaves, and seeds— for treating many ills. The Latin word *rosmarinus* is no doubt an etymological reinterpretation of *rhops myrinos*, a Greek name meaning something akin to "sweet-smelling shrub." Widely dispersed throughout the untamed thickets of the Mediterranean, the plant has been cultivated in gardens since antiquity.

In Roman times rosemary was found not only in vegetable and herb gardens, but even more importantly in the park-type landscapes that provided rest and spiritual renewal for the fortunate landowners. The aromatically fragrant plant was said to stimulate mental acuity and memory in those who lingered in the charming peace of the garden. One ancient author described the experience of a garden stroll as being surrounded by pleasant fragrances that cause neither headache nor sensual overstimulation, but instead promote health and mental acuity.

Dioscorides, physician and pharmacologist, recommended rosemary branches boiled in water as a cure for jaundice. After drinking the beverage, he suggested that the patient would be further fortified by bodily exercise, baths, and a glass of wine (3.89).

The gentleman farmer Columella, who has given us so much insight into everyday country life in antiquity, placed his beehives close to blossoming rosemary shrubs to improve the quality of his honey (*On agriculture* 9.4). In autumn he prepared a wine spiced with the juices extracted from sprigs of rosemary, which was left to ferment in an amphora for two months. He failed to reveal, unfortunately, the type of ailment he intended to treat with this brew made from two urns of juice and one-and-a-half pounds of rosemary (*On agriculture* 12.36).

Unlike today, ancient cookery appears to have made no use of rosemary. Perhaps it was too closely associated with the gods to be profaned as a flavoring herb in everyday use.

Rosemary *Rosmarinus officinalis* (Lamiaceae)
Nees van Esenbeck, no. 162

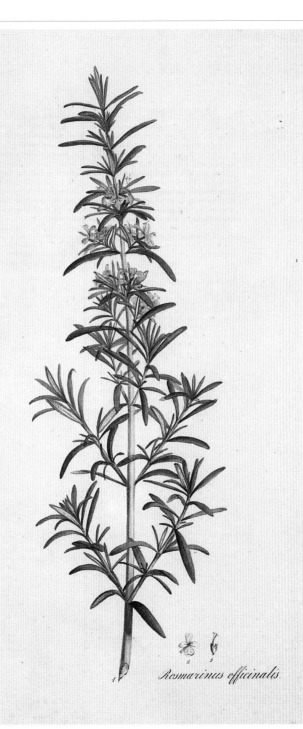

Rosmarinus officinalis.

rue

In antiquity rue was considered one of their best medicinal and kitchen herbs. The undersides of its decoratively feathery leaves contain glands that produce an oil that was considered as essential to health as its darkly spicy-tasting greens were essential to the culinary arts.

The effects of rue have inspired many stories. Because of its ascribed magical powers, it came into wide use as an ingredient in medications and tinctures for illnesses—especially for the bites by poisonous beasts. As if to confirm this, Pliny passed along a story that weasels protected themselves by eating rue before they battled poisonous snakes (*Natural History* 20.51). Whoever rubbed himself with the juice of rue —or carried only a sprig of the plant on his person— would supposedly not be stung by either hornet or scorpion (*Natural History* 20.51). Snakes were believed to flee from the smoke of burning rue.

Rue was found so effective in strengthening eyesight that painters and jewel carvers ate it, combined with garden cress (most likely *Nasturtium officinale*) and bread, to maintain the visual acuity so essential to their occupations.

According to ancient household medical practice, rue sprigs stanched nosebleeds, and the herb served to clean the teeth. For earache one dripped the juice into the ear. Epileptics drank the juice of boiled rue to help when shaking became intolerable before a seizure. "Juice made from grated rue and vinegar is applied in droplets to the temples or on the skull of the insane," Pliny reported, adding that "among all plants of the garden, rue is the only one that is also frequently used in illnesses of cattle" (*Natural History* 20.51).

For preservation, rue was laid in a tub, sprinkled with salt, and left to sweat for two days in the shade. Once it had released sufficient liquid to be submerged in its own juices, it was washed, placed in a pot, and salts and vinegar were poured over it. Along with dried bunches of fennel, the rue was pressed down by a heavy weight so that the juices rose to the rim of the pot. Before use, it was rinsed in water or wine and garnished with olive oil.

One day when he decided to treat his friends to a lavish and delicious meal, the poet Martial began with an appetizer of roast tuna fish garnished with boiled eggs and rue leaves.

Rue was known to thrive in sun and dry soil, but wither in soggy, severe winters or overly rich soil. It requires fertilizing with ash and prospers best beneath a fig tree, according to ancient gardeners. A rue shrub would flourish for many years—as long as it was not touched by a woman who was menstruating.

RUE *Ruta graveolens* (Rutaceae)
Nees van Esenbeck, no. 376

Ruta graveolens

sage

Grown worldwide, the different varieties of sage have a whole range of uses and blossoms of widely varying colors, but their leaves all contain active ingredients that were prized equally for ancient Chinese medicine and for the healing rituals of the Aztecs of Mexico. However, when Carolus Linnaeus devised his system for botany in 1735, he chose the genus name *Salvia* that was used by classical authors in the first century A.D. *Salvia* now encompasses the entire genus, but it was originally more restricted in use: Roman herbalists coined it for only one variety of sage, native to southern Europe, today's *Salvia officinalis*.

Theophrastos and Hippocrates supplied its first descriptions in the fourth century B.C., calling it *elelisphakos* (or *elaphoboskon*; Greek meaning "deer fodder"). Differentiating between the wild and cultivated forms, they described a medically and cosmetically usable plant with agreeably aromatic leaves that felt like a ragged old garment to the touch.

The essential oils, tannins, and bitters contained in the leaves are in fact effective for treating inflammations. In antiquity a liquid was extracted from leaves, stalks, and branches and used as a styptic and a diuretic, as well as for cosmetic hair treatment. It was believed that hair could be dyed darker with sage, that it promoted growth, and gave hair—particularly dark hair—a brilliant sheen. Greek herbalists counseled cooking sage leaves in wine, so that a treatment for flatulence and digestive problems was always conveniently available in the household.

Roman literature has surprisingly little to say about sage. Columella, Martial, Ovid, and Cicero—usually so eloquent—seem to have been ignorant or unenthusiastic about the plant. In the following terse note on its effects, Pliny was the first to use the name *salvia*: "Our herbal experts today cite a plant as *elelisphakos* in Greek and *salvia* in Latin, which resembles mint but has a gray tint and pleasant fragrance. They expel a dead fetus by placing leaves on the body, and also use it to drive worms out of the ears and abscesses" (*Natural History* 22.71). Centuries later, his use of the term *salvia* appears to have stimulated the imagination of those monks who copied the ancient manuscripts in medieval cloisters, thus saving them for posterity. They ascribed immense powers to a particular plant whose name derived, they said, from the Latin *salvare* (to heal). Every medieval monastery garden cultivated sage for its fragrant evergreen leaves, a quality that implied divine healing and eternal youth.

By the tenth century, in the first western school of medicine established in Salerno, Italy, it was written: "Wherefore should a man die, if sage grows in his garden?"

COMMON SAGE *Salvia officinalis* (Lamiaceae)
Nees van Esenbeck, no. 161

Salvia officinalis

spearmint

Gardeners of antiquity apparently valued a rich assortment of fragrant mints in their herbal beds. Ancient texts and medieval herbals report that gardeners cultivated the varieties horsemint (*Mentha longifolia*), watermint (*Mentha aquatica*), and spearmint (*Mentha spicata*). Unknown then, today's highly popular peppermint (*Mentha × piperita*) was not in existence until 1696, when it was hybridized in England from the closely related horsemint and watermint.

There is not an ancient author concerned with nature and medicine who did not describe and attempt to classify the wealth of varieties of mints that developed under cultivation. Mints are rich in essential oils, especially menthol, which has pain-relieving and tonic properties. Crowns made of mint branches were very popular in antiquity; they adorned the wearer with a handsome head ornament and additionally gave off a pleasant fragrance that proved effective at dispersing wine odors at banquets. Mint was also believed to be an aphrodisiac, and garlands woven from these plants were sometimes called "Corona Veneris"—crown of Venus, with her association to love.

Mint had religious significance in the rustic cults of the gods of vegetation and fertility. The earth mother Ceres (Demeter) set off in desperate pursuit of her daughter Proserpina (Persephone), a captive of Pluto (Hades, the god of the Underworld). Before leaving she was served a puree of mint, flour, and water—a recipe that continued to have an honored place among the mysterious rites at Demeter's sanctuary in Eleusis. Indeed, according to the mythology of mint's origin, in a fit of jealousy and hatred, Persephone, goddess of the Underworld, transformed the nymph Mentha into a fragrant mint plant because she was the beloved of Pluto.

The Roman poet Ovid gives us a glimpse of everyday life in antiquity in his touching tale of the visit by the gods Jupiter and Mercury to the elderly married couple Philemon and Baucis. Before serving their simple meal, Baucis cleaned the table with fresh mint sprigs from her garden—a humble act that was richly rewarded (Ovid *Metamorphoses* 8.661–64). Pliny did report that the pleasant fragrance of mint was indispensable at any festive country meal.

Columella, the Spanish-born Roman gentleman, presented a recipe for a green sauce for roast meats, which drew upon various types of mint. It became a precursor to pesto, the sauce from Italy that is so wildly popular today: in a mortar thoroughly grind savory, mint, rue, coriander, celery, chives, arugula, green thyme, and pennyroyal, add grated walnuts to taste, and mix in pepper, vinegar, and oil (Columella *On agriculture* 12.59). The mint sauce that often accompanies lamb today may have originated from a recipe like this one.

SPEARMINT *Mentha spicata* (Lamiaceae)
Nees van Esenbeck, no. 167

Mentha viridis

st.-john's-wort

If you rub or crush the shiny dark-yellow blossoms covered with black dots and variegated stripes, the St.-John's-wort shown here (and a few of its relatives) will emit a blood-red liquid. Accordingly, in antiquity the plant was called "man's blood," among other names, and great supernatural powers were attributed to it. The gushing bright red juice is a strong-scented resin that was put to medicinal use very early. Its healing powers reside not just in the blossoms but also in the leaves, which appear perforated because of its prominent oil glands—thus the reason for its specific epithet, *perforatum* (punctured). For centuries its leaves and blossoms were collected around the time of summer solstice, and since this season peaks on the twenty-first of June—Saint John's Day—the plant was so named in English-speaking countries.

The different species of *Hypericum* can vary markedly in appearance and show unusual ecological adaptability. We find members of the genus scattered from East Asia all the way to North America, where *Hypericum perforatum*, the European native, has long been naturalized and to an extent has become an irksome weed. Outside the garden the plant thrives in dry soil and narrow sites along paths, roadways, and abandoned fields.

The Greek Dioscorides enumerated several varieties of the plant, all with similar medicinal effects, but recommended the seed of *Hypericum perforatum* and *Hypericum coris* (from Ischia, an island near Naples). He stressed the need to take this medicine for fourteen days to achieve a cure. Even today St.-John's-wort is considered quite a good alternative treatment for rheumatism, arthritis, and aching muscles. Moreover, St.-John's-wort is a popular remedy for anxiety and depression. This may have been known to Dioscorides, who wrote that its roots, cooked in wine, could restore an exhausted patient to his original "liveliness." While ingesting the liquid, the patient should be sure to bundle up warmly, as heavy perspiration enhances the desired effect (Dioscorides 3.172). Although modern medical research has extensively studied the effectiveness of this important old healing plant, the actual curative mechanisms are not yet fully explained.

Long ago, as today, oil from the plant was good for burns and other skin injuries, perhaps one of the reasons why *Hypericum* was cultivated in Roman-conquered settlements and near fortresses in northern Europe, as confirmed by archaeological finds from tombs.

In an ancient villa in Oplontis, on the Gulf of Naples, remnants of St.-John's-wort have been discovered in carbonized hay, where its tough stalks may not have been a very welcome component. The stalks did, however, possibly give rise to its nickname, "hardhay."

HARDHAY *Hypericum perforatum* (Clusiaceae)
Nees van Esenbeck, no. 420

94

Hypericum perforatum.

thyme

"Everyone knows thyme," wrote the physician Dioscorides in the first line of his discourse on the pharmacological value of this very aromatic herb—the subject supported by more than three millennia of experience.

Then as now, people resorted to thyme to control coughs by boiling it with honey or vinegar and thus activating the essential oil with its strong-acting thymol. The product eased the cramping cough and promoted circulation of blood to the skin. Thyme's valuable properties also had a favorable effect on a stomach subject to frequent cramping. According to Dioscorides, thyme was used to treat asthma and loosen congestion in the throat and stomach. Thyme's leaves are rich in essential oils, tannic acids, and aromatic compounds known as flavonoids.

Perennial thyme belongs to the Lamiaceae family, and flourishes in a dry, sunny site that approximates its comfortable native habitat in the Mediterranean. The thyme-covered slopes of Hymettos near Athens have become famous. However, it is easier to harvest its fresh sprigs all summer long when it is nurtured in a kitchen garden, where it is a necessity. It is most flavorful just before blossoming. Patience is a prerequisite for stripping the tiny, fragrant leaves for use when they are needed.

Crowns of thyme were a very popular adornment for revelers at festive banquets. What truly mattered in antiquity, however, was the scent of thyme rising from altars to please the gods. The intensity of this aroma, heightened by burning, may also account for its name, because the Greek word *thymon* refers not only to this plant but also to heart, flame, vital energy, passion, and smoke.

Not only pleasant to smell, the fumes from burning thyme were thought to have an antiseptic effect: Before the onset of winter the ancient beekeeper would smoke his hives with thyme to keep them free of vermin. Gentlemen farmers like the poet Virgil or the naturalist Pliny recommended that their gardener-readers plant thyme beds close to their hives. Most importantly, because bees are so attracted to the pink-violet or white blossoms of thyme, they produced both the thyme honey that has been famous for centuries and the rich earnings it could generate. Pliny noted the tastiness and beneficial effects of thyme honey.

The pungent-sweet scent, slender branches, and light but robust blossoms offer a fine contrast to all varieties of rose blossoms and, when arranged together in a rush basket, made a very welcome gift to Venus, goddess of love.

In all periods thyme has been a welcome guest in the kitchen. Dioscorides valued the herb thusly: "It finds distinguished uses as the healthy man's seasoning"(3.44).

THYME *Thymus vulgaris* and
WILD THYME *Thymus serpyllum* (Lamiaceae)
Nees van Esenbeck, no. 181

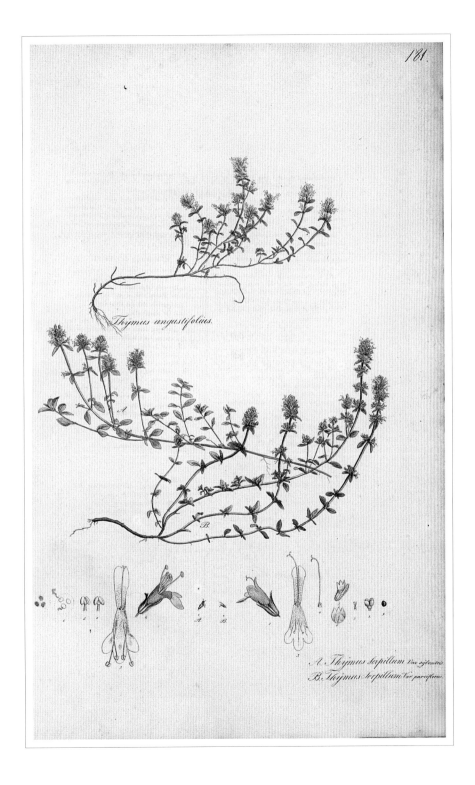

Thymus angustifolius.

A. *Thymus serpillum* Var. *sylvestris*
B. *Thymus serpillum* Var. *parviflorus.*

ACKNOWLEDGMENTS

The idea for this book was first proposed by Marion True, former Curator of Antiquities at the Getty Museum; I am very grateful to her for her strong support of this project. Landscape architect Denis Kurutz, who led the team that designed the gardens at the Getty Villa in Malibu, was an essential helper in sharing his ideas of ancient herb gardening. I owe thanks to Professor H. W. Lack and Dr. B. Mory for their generous support and collegial help. The library of the German Archaeological Institute in Rome provided an important venue for work. My gratitude is due to Mark Greenberg, Editor in Chief of Getty Publications, for agreeing to undertake this project. David Baker's sensitive translation rendered my text into fluent English, and Louise Barber edited it with great expertise. Benedicte Gilman, Senior Editor in Getty Publications, guided the project with patience from start to finish.

M. H.

A Note on Illustrations

The botanical drawings in this book are reproduced by permission of Dr. Norbert Kilian from publications in the library of the Botanischer Garten and Botanisches Museum, Freie Universität Berlin. The author has photographed them all. Most of the drawings are from Theodor Friedrich Ludwig Nees van Esenbeck, *Plantae medicinales, oder, Sammlung offizineller Pflanzen* (Düsseldorf, 1828).

The illustration of celery is from Friedrich Gottlob Hayne, *Getreue Darstellung und Beschreibung der in der Arzneikunde gebräuchlichen Gewächse* (Berlin, 1805–); myrtle is from Diedrich Franz Leonhard von Schlechtendal, *Flora von Deutschland*, vol. 22 (Berlin, 1885); and Cretan dittany is from William Curtis, *The Botanical Magazine*, vol. 9 (London, 1795) while iris is from his vol. 16 (1803).

Some of the botanical drawings were inscribed with Latin names that are no longer used. The more modern names are used in the text.

Suggestions for Further Reading

Bowe, Patrick. *Gardens of the Roman World*. Los Angeles, 2004.

Carroll, Maureen. *Earthly Paradises: Ancient Gardens in History and Archaeology*. Los Angeles, 2003.

Ciarallo, Annamaria. *Gardens of Pompeii*. Los Angeles, 2003.

The Greek Herbal of Dioscorides. Illustrated by a Byzantine A.D. 512. Englished by John Goodyer, A.D. 1655. Edited and first printed A.D. 1933 by Robert T. Gunther. London, 1968.

Farrar, Linda. *Ancient Roman Gardens*. Phoenix Mill, Thrup, Stroud, Gloucestershire, 1998.

Jashemski, Wilhelmina F. *The Gardens of Pompeii, Herculaneum, and the Villas Destroyed by Vesuvius*. New Rochelle, NY, 1979 (vol. 1) and 1993 (vol. 2).

Jashemski, Wilhelmina F. *A Pompeian Herbal: Ancient and Modern Medicinal Plants*. Austin, 1999.

Leach, H. "On the Origins of Kitchen Gardening in the Ancient Near East." *Garden History* 10.1 (1982): 1–16.

Macdougall, Elizabeth B., ed. *Ancient Roman Villa Gardens*. Dumbarton Oaks Colloquium on the History of Landscape Architecture, vol. 10. Washington, D.C., 1987.

Macdougall, Elizabeth B., and Wilhelmina F. Jashemski, eds. *Ancient Roman Gardens*. Dumbarton Oaks Colloquium on the History of Landscape Architecture, vol. 7. Washington, D.C., 1981.

Meyer, Frederick G. "Food Plants Identified from Carbonized Remains at Pompeii and Other Vesuvian Sites." In *Studia Pompeiana & Classica in Honor of Wilhelmina Jashemski*, vol. 1. Edited by Robert I. Curtis. New Rochelle, NY, 1988.

Zohary, Daniel, and Maria Hopf. *Domestication of Plants in the Old World*. 3rd edition. Oxford, 2000.

Getty Publications
1200 Getty Center Drive, Suite 500
Los Angeles, California 90049-1682
www.getty.edu

Mark Greenberg, *Editor in Chief*

David J. Baker, *Translator*
Louise D. Barber, *Manuscript Editor*
Benedicte Gilman, *Editorial Coordinator*
Richard Naskali, *Botanical Consultant*
Agnes Anderson, *Designer*
Pamela Heath and Elizabeth Zozom, *Production Coordinators*

Printed in Singapore by Tien Wah Press

Library of Congress Cataloging-in-Publication Data

Heilmeyer, Marina.
  Ancient herbs / Marina Heilmeyer ; [David J. Baker, translator].
    p. cm.
  ISBN-13: 978-0-89236-884-6 (hardcover)
  1. Herbs. 2. Cookery (Herbs) 3. Herbs—Therapeutic use. I. Title.
  SB351.H5H3413 2007
  581.6'303—dc22

                    2006030770

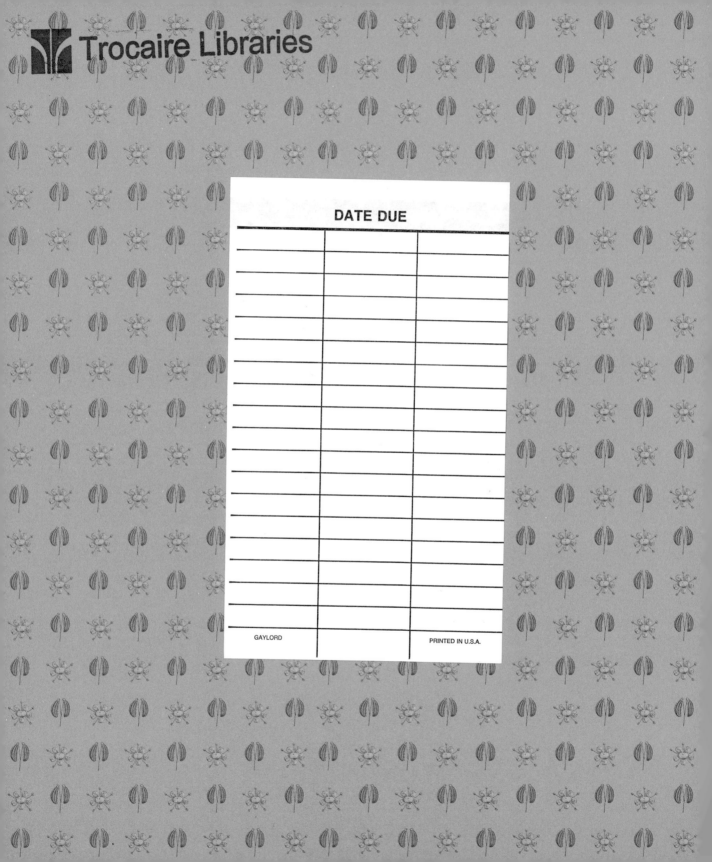

Trocaire Libraries

DATE DUE

GAYLORD   PRINTED IN U.S.A.